# Hidden Power

# Hidden Power

## The Seniority System
### and Other Customs of Congress

### MAURICE B. TOBIN
Edited by Joan Shaffer

Contributions in Political Science, Number 155

**Greenwood Press**
New York • Westport, Connecticut • London

**Library of Congress Cataloging-in-Publication Data**

Tobin, Maurice B.
    Hidden power.

    (Contributions in political science, ISSN 0147-1066 ;
no. 155)
    Bibliography: p.
    Includes index.
    1. United States.  Congress—Committees—Seniority
system.  I. Shaffer, Joan.  II. Title.  III. Series.
JK1029.2.T63  1986       328.73'076        85-30217
ISBN 0-313-25342-0 (lib. bdg. : alk. paper)

Library of Congress Catalog Card Number: 85-30217
ISBN: 0-313-25342-0
ISSN: 0147-1066

First published in 1986

Greenwood Press, Inc.
88 Post Road West, Westport, Connecticut 06881

Printed in the United States of America

The paper used in this book complies with the
Permanent Paper Standard issued by the National
Information Standards Organization (Z39.48-1984).

10 9 8 7 6 5 4 3 2 1

To my wife, Joan, whose knowledge of politics and whose wisdom contributed greatly to this work.

To our children, Alexis Dorette and Ian Maurice, with the hope that they will get to know and respect Congress as we do.

# Contents

# Acknowledgments

I would like to thank Joan Shaffer, my editor, who tirelessly edited, researched, wrote, rewrote, and still stayed in good humor.

Thanks also go to Seldon Wallace for her ideas and encouragement, to Harriett Robnett for her research and good will, to Jim Davidson for his numerous contributions, to Timothy Dickenson for agreeably arguing, as usual, and to Carol Crespo, my crisis manager, who was loyal and faithful beyond words.

All proceeds from this book will be turned over to the Tobin Foundation, a non-profit organization, 1850 K Street, N.W., Washington, D.C. 20006.

# Introduction

The congressional seniority system, not mandated by the Constitution or the rules of Congress, and never voted upon in our democracy, nevertheless represented great power for over half a century. The Congress, a coequal branch of our government, was conceived by the Founding Fathers to serve a representative function. Each state would have two Senators and at least one member of the House of Representatives. To ensure that all citizens had equal voice, each Senator and House member would have one vote of equal value. In theory.

However, when practice evolves into custom and then becomes tradition, it can be many times more immovable than law, and such is the case with the congressional seniority system. It has been and still is controversial. Some say seniority encourages autocratic rule, the antithesis of democratic government; yet others hold that rigid adherence to seniority is the only way to prevent Congress from descending into chaos. This book is about that once inviolate but now greatly weakened system and other rules and customs of Congress that affect its power structure.

Charles de Gaulle once said, "How can you govern a country that has two-hundred-fifty-six different kinds of cheese?" The questions that occurred to me while writing this book were similar: How can the Speaker of the House really control 434 independent Congressmen? Is it possible for the Senate Majority Leader to create a cohesive voting bloc when he must do so with more than fifty Senators, each with a separate agenda and serving a different constituency? Is it possible to preserve party order and loyalty when each member must satisfy different voters to ensure his or her own reelection?

Today the Congress seems relatively paralyzed; and to a large degree it is because the seniority system and the rules related to it, which for so long guaranteed order in the congressional process, are no longer in place, creating an operational vacuum. Seniority and power were for many years synonymous in the Congress, and were held principally by Southerners. Although it is argued that seniority smothered initiative, it also—rightly or wrongly—gave an unalterable and functional structure to Congress. An institution that cost a billion dollars to run in 1984 and whose budget keeps growing is of serious concern to the taxpayers, most particularly if that institution passes the laws governing the collection and appropriation of the nation's income.

Congressional leaders are further concerned that in the first session of the 99th Congress, some 70 percent of the 189 laws enacted were considered "non-substantive or administrative"—for example, Made in America Day, Baltic Freedom Day, National Organ Donation Awareness Week, George Milligan Control Tower Day, etc.[1] Senator David Pryor (D., Arkansas) is one of the members of Congress concerned not only about lack of substance but also the time wasted as a result. "How," asks the Senator, "can such an institution so rich in tradition and costing a billion dollars a year to operate spend about three months of the year calling quorum and roll calls?"[2]

Would the reinstatement of powerful "ring bearers," as Senator John Warner (R., Virginia) calls the major committee chairmen, make Congress run more effectively? Does an entrenched staffing and subcommittee system make that impossible? Before Congress enters its 100th session, and in the face of the upcoming 1986 elections, many of its members are seeking answers to these questions.

Seniority may or may not confer wisdom, but it does promote experience and establish channels of working authority. A Congress without a seniority system or some alternative that works is one without order and one in which there will be the most intense personal competition among members. "Keep politics out of politics" may sound incongruous, but even in politics, politics must have its proper place.

Over sixty Washington power holders—current and former Senators, Congressmen, Cabinet members, White House officials, and journalists—were interviewed for this book. They give their thoughts, their recommendations, and their recollections and I have, as much as possible, let the original sources speak for themselves. Direct quotes in the text are from these interviews unless otherwise noted. A listing of the interviews is included in the Bibliography. The issues of power and change that I have addressed have resulted in the present form of the seniority system—and will, to a large extent, determine the future structure of Congress.

## Notes

1. Senate Democratic Policy Committee compilation of Public Laws of the 99th Congress, January 3, 1985 to December 9, 1985, 1st sess.

2. Senator Pryor has outlined some of the time wasting procedures of the first session of the 99th Congress in *Congressional Record*, 99th Cong., 2d sess., October 31, 1985, S 14491–14499 and December 19, 1985, S 18169.

# Hidden Power

# 1

# A View Over Time: Seniority, the Unwritten Law

The seniority system was not devised in Independence Hall. It was unheard of until about a century ago. And then it took another fifty years for it to become a crucial issue.
—Congressman Morris Udall

Seniority is the key to power in the United States Congress: length of service determines committee rank and the committees control legislation. The most power, naturally, resides with the chairman, the member of the majority party who has the longest unbroken committee tenure.

Committee status based on length of service has rarely been violated even though no rule mandates this procedure; rather, seniority emerged out of necessity and custom. The rules state merely that each house shall determine committee membership and chairmen.

House of Representatives Rule X says that "at the commencement of each Congress, the House shall elect as chairman of each standing committee one of the members thereof. . . . All vacancies in the standing committees of the House shall be filled by election by the House." Senate Rule XXIV states that "the appointment of standing committees in the Senate, unless otherwise ordered, shall proceed by ballot to appoint severally the chairmen of each committee, and then by one ballot, the other members necessary to complete the same." (The Senate rule was changed in 1979 to read: "In the appointment of the standing committees, or to fill vacancies thereon, the Senate, unless otherwise ordered, shall by resolution appoint the chairman of each such committee and the other members thereof. On the demand of any Senator, a separate vote shall be had on the appointment of the chairman and of any such committee and on the appointment of the other members thereof. Each such resolution shall be subject to amendment and to division of the question.")

The House began establishing standing committees during the First Congress, 1789–1791, and the Senate soon followed, basing its system on that of the House. At the time, seniority was unimportant—no one had any—and each body determined its method of selection.

### Committee Assignment Authority: The House

In the House of Representatives the authority to assign membership, both majority and minority, and designate chairmen was vested in the Speaker of the House. The Constitution provides that the House appoint a Speaker, but does not define the role; consequently, the Speaker's powers—both stated and implied—depend on the authority he chooses to wield and the cooperation given him by the members of the House.

The earliest usage of the term "speaker" was in reference to the 14th century English Parliament and the role was defined as an impartial interpreter of the will of the legislative body (the House of Commons) to its superior (the Crown). This definition fits the early role of the Speaker when he was both the presiding officer of the House and a passive liaison between the President and the Congress.

It was not until Henry Clay of Kentucky[1] assumed the speakership in 1811 that the office became distinctly partisan. Clay radically transformed the role of the Speaker, serving as both presiding officer and leader of the majority. The Speaker's greatest power, however, was his authority to make committee appointments. This power remained with the Speaker, unchallenged, until 1910–1911 when insurgents of both parties revolted against Speaker Joseph G. Cannon, a ten-term conservative from Illinois, appointed Speaker in 1903, who used his powers of committee appointment to create majorities to pass legislation he favored. He ignored seniority, appointing as chairmen only those who agreed with him, even placing friends as chairmen of committees on which they had not previously served.

Cannon used his powers of recognition on the floor and as chairman of the Rules Committee to control all legislation. This lasted until 1910 when his abuses provoked rebellion. The Speaker's power to make committee assignments then was wrenched from Cannon and given to a Democratic Committee on Committees, composed of all Democrats on the Ways and Means Committee and chaired by the Majority Leader. The Democrats' system was continued when the Republicans gained power six years later; however, their Committee on Committees was composed of one Congressman from each state that elected a Republican to the House.

The procedure at the beginning of each new Congress required the two parties' Committees on Committees to select committee membership and chairmen, followed by a confirmation vote of the entire House. It should be noted, however, that ratification by the entire House was merely *pro forma*, and chairmanships always went to the most senior member of the majority party in the House.

### Committee Assignment Authority: The Senate

In the Senate, the seniority system took hold much earlier and held faster. One reason may have been that the Senate had no powerful central leader, comparable to the House Speaker, to control committee assignments and chairmanships.

Before the Senate establihed its first eleven standing committees in 1816, every piece of legislation necessitated a new committee, to be dissolved at the end of each Congress. Chairmanships were rotated, and until 1823, committee membership was selected by the entire Senate, voting from the floor. This proved too time-consuming and cumbersome so different methods were tried, including giving authority to the President Pro Tempore and the Presiding Officer. Because none of these methods was satisfactory, the Senate, without opposition, adopted the seniority system in 1846. At the beginning of each session of Congress, the Republican and Democratic Committees on Committees would draw up slates that were voted upon by the full Senate.

The seniority criterion rarely was breached for over a century, requiring, as in the House, junior members to accept assignments

to such "minor" committees as District of Columbia and Post Office, while senior members served on important ones like Foreign
Relations and Appropriations. The first weakening of the seniority
system in the Senate came in 1953 when Senator Lyndon B. Johnson
of Texas, newly chosen leader of the Senate Democrats, instituted
what came to be known as the Johnson Rule[2] which specified that
each Democratic Senator be assigned to one major committee before any Democrat is assigned to a second major committee.

However, pressure to modify the seniority system increased in
the 1960s, and in 1971 the Senate Democrats, the party in power,
ruled that any Democratic Senator would be free to challenge the
nomination of a committee chairman.

## Seniority and Powerful Committee Chairmen

As noted, seniority evolved because of the need for an efficient
and automatic method of organizing and determining status, and
stayed firmly entrenched until the reform movements of the 1960s
and 1970s.[3] Under the seniority system, committee chairmen were
beholden to no one, save their constituents, and were not obli-
gated to pass their party's programs, support the leadership, or
share power with junior members. The absolute control a chairman could exercise over his committee left other committee members with little option but to ratify the chairman's decisions. Junior
members, with the least legislative influence, lacked good committee assignments and had little opportunity to participate in committee work.

The principal beneficiaries of a dislodgment of seniority as the
sole criterion for determining committee rank, aside from junior
members, would be the political parties. Party control of the legislative process is denied by seniority because a chairman is not
required to support his party's position. Rather, sequential reelection, often determined by a small portion of the population, be-
stows legislative power. Party loyalty is not a requisite attribute.

Critics found more fault with seniority than the lack of partisan
purity, charging that seniority was a stagnant deterrent to parliamentary enlightenment, an obstacle to progress, and a tool for pre-
serving tyranny by a minority while sanctifying longevity and even
senility.

Yet, for decades, the seniority system held fast, its defenders pointing out that automatic elevation of the most senior member eliminated competitive struggles detrimental to congressional harmony. In addition, prearranged selection prevented effective pressure from being applied by special interest groups. Thus, seniority could be lauded as the embodiment of democracy's finest attributes, bringing purity to the process and assuring that the chairman, due to tenure, would always possess the greatest legislative experience, the most in-depth knowledge of his committee's subject matter, and be the least susceptible to transient political surges.

Besides, if seniority were to be abolished, former Majority Leader Alben W. Barkley of Kentucky warned, "the element of favoritism would come into play, and there would be logrolling and electioneering for the votes of the committee members by those who wanted to be committee chairmen. . . . Jealousies, ambitions, and the frailties of human nature would crop up in the electioneering methods of men who wanted to be chairmen of committees."[4]

Seniority rarely was overruled until the 1970s except in certain instances where party loyalty was openly ignored. Two Democrats, a Senator and a Congressman, lost their seniority during the 89th Congress when they opposed their party's choice for President, Lyndon Johnson, and supported Barry Goldwater.[5]

Seniority could also be lost if a member switched parties, as in the cases of Senators Wayne Morse of Oregon and Strom Thurmond of South Carolina.[6]

## Pressure for Reform

By the end of the 1960s both the mood of the country and the composition of the Congress had changed, creating a fertile climate for a shift in power. Dissatisfaction with Congress was increasing and, according to a Harris poll, only 26 percent of the population approved of Congress in 1971. In contrast, Harris' 1965 polls had shown Congress with an approval rating of 64 percent. The House had changed, too: half its membership had arrived in 1967 or later and an overwhelming majority—316 members out of 435—had been elected after 1960. The power holders, the committee chairmen who had come to Congress in the 1930s and 1940s, were about fourteen years older than the average Congressman.

However, but for a few exceptions, seniority remained unshaken until liberal and moderate House Democrats joined to form the Democratic Study Group (DSG) in the late 1960s and pushed through the first fundamental changes in House rules in half a century. The DSG dedicated its efforts to a revival of the Democratic Caucus, the organized body of all House Democrats, as the basic determinant of Democratic policy and organization in the House. Through the Caucus the DSG made inroads on the seniority system by instituting an automatic secret ballot vote on chairmen at the start of each Congress.

The Caucus had gradually fallen into disuse since 1920, and by the 1950s its main function was to meet once each Congress to elect the Democratic leadership and, when in the majority, such other House officers as the Sergeant at Arms and Parliamentarian. But the DSG pressed on, and in January 1969, it won a rules change requiring monthly Caucus meetings. Even more important, the Caucus took control over committee assignments and could veto the choices made by the Committee on Committees.

Pressure for reform was coming from outside the Congress as well, and in the late 1960s such organizations as the United Auto Workers, the AFL-CIO, and the Americans for Democratic Action began to demand changes. Foremost in the reform drive was Common Cause, the "citizens' lobby," which pushed for the abolition of the seniority system. Common Cause proposed that "each committee and subcommittee chairman must be elected at the beginning of each new Congress or when a vacancy occurs by open ballot [later changed to supporting secret ballot] of the full membership of the majority party of each house of Congress. Ranking minority party members should be chosen by the same procedure in the minority party caucus." Common Cause President Fred Wertheimer, who was its executive vice-president during the 1970s, said that "the fight for seniority reform was really a fight to strengthen the leadership and to strengthen the accountability of committee chairmen. . . . The arbitrariness of the seniority system led to the arbitrariness by committee chairmen."

Although pressure was on the Democrats, the majority party, it was the Republican Conference, the counterpart to the Democratic Caucus, that took the first step to loosen the seniority system's absolute hold when it adopted a proposal in 1969 that required secret ballot election of each ranking minority member.

The first major effort to inject a measure of accountability into the selection of committee chairmen occurred in January 1971 when a reform committee organized by the Democratic Caucus in the late 1960s under Julia Hansen of Washington issued its recommendations. These were approved by the Caucus and implemented in the 92nd Congress. Only one challenge was brought, and that unsuccessful—against John McMillan of South Carolina, chairman of the District of Columbia Committee—but it was the first time the seniority system was seriously threatened.

The Caucus continued to push for more reform, and a rule was adopted in 1971 providing that the Committee on Committees need not follow seniority when recommending committee chairmen. This was the first Caucus assertion that seniority not be the sole criterion for chairmanship determination. In another weakening of the powers of chairmen, the Caucus adopted a rule permitting a separate vote on any chairman if ten members of that committee demanded it. However, if there were no challenges, the most senior member would become chairman automatically, as was usually the case. Another Hansen reform stipulated that House members could be entitled to only one subcommittee chairmanship. This rules change opened up subcommittee chairmanships to younger members.

The pressure continued. The year 1972 was an election year and Common Cause took the congressional reform movement to the national conventions. The Democrats endorsed Common Cause's proposal to end seniority; the Republicans did not, although some GOP delegates pressed for its passage.

The second set of reforms, "Hansen II," introduced at the beginning of the 93rd Congress (January 1973) again weakened the seniority system. The 240-member Democratic Caucus met on the House floor behind closed doors and ruled that a secret ballot vote would be taken on any committee chairman if requested by one-fifth of the members present. Further, the Democratic Committee on Committees was expanded to include the Democratic leadership. The Speaker, the Majority Leader, and the Caucus chairman were added to the committee, and the Speaker, rather than the chairman of Ways and Means, became its head.

For two days the meeting continued and the Democratic Caucus voted, alphabetically by committee. All committee chairmen were endorsed; yet opposition votes were cast against six of the twenty-one chairmen by more than 20 percent of the members.[7]

Majority Leader Thomas P. O'Neill of Massachusetts had proposed the secret ballot to protect challengers against possible reprisals, but all members did not support the provision. Chet Holifield of California, for example, under challenge by Benjamin S. Rosenthal of New York for his chairmanship of Government Operations, said: "If I'm going to be stabbed in the back then I want it to be done openly." Holifield won his chairmanship, but could not defeat the secret ballot rule. This change in the rules modified the behavior of the committee chairman, explains House committee staffer and former Senate aide Mace Broide. "The 'new breed' of committee chairman," Broide says, "is no different from the 'old breed'. The only difference is that the new chairman is tempered by the knowledge that the Caucus can unseat him. He must be less autocratic and more accommodating than in the past."

The Hansen II reforms also brought about what is called the Subcommittee Bill of Rights that allowed the Caucus to vote on subcommittee chairmen and provided for larger budgets and staffs for subcommittees, further dispersing power within the House.

Seniority was weakened by other rules changes adopted by the Caucus: one major committee assignment would be given to every Congressman requesting it; each member could request a subcommittee assignment of his choice; and no Congressman would be allowed to serve on more than one major committee.

The third set of proposals from the Hansen Committee, "Hansen III," recommended that the Steering and Policy Committee act as the Committee on Committees, thus stripping Ways and Means of its committee assignment authority.[8] It also changed the complicated balloting process for electing committee chairmen by allowing nominations to be made from the floor of the Caucus meeting if the Steering and Policy Committee recommendations were overruled. In addition, the Hansen III proposals required that the Appropriations Committee subcommittee chairs be voted upon in the same manner as the chairmen of the standing committees.

Then Hansen III, in another move specifically aimed at the pow-

erful Ways and Means Committee, directed that standing committees with more than fifteen members have at least four subcommittees. This provision established six subcommittees for Ways and
Means, which previously had none. A final erosion of Ways and
Means' power was the creation of the Budget Committee to coor-
dinate revenues (Ways and Means' jurisdiction) and expenses (Appropriations' jurisdiction) of the federal government. Proclaiming
he was "wildly happy at what we've done," DSG Chairman Philip
Burton of California said, "We're finally getting somewhere."

However, the Democratic Caucus voted down two much stronger
restrictions on the seniority system: one requiring committee leaders to retire at age seventy and one limiting them to no more than
three terms, both proposals that would have substantially modified
the seniority system.

### Three House Chairmen Overthrown

When the 94th Congress organized in January 1975, three House
Democrats entitled by seniority to committee chairs were defeated, and a fourth, Wayne Hays of Ohio, only narrowly retained
the chairmanship of the House Administration Committee. The three
chairmen were F. Edward Hebert of Louisiana, denied the Armed
Services Committee; Wright Patman of Texas, denied Banking and
Currency; and William Poage of Texas, denied Agriculture. Although all had been accused of autocratic behavior, it should be
noted that the defeated chairmen broke with no congressional norms,
did not change party, nor did they overtly support a presidential
candidate of the opposing party. Rather there was a general mood
of reform combined with an increase in junior membership and
younger Congressmen who wanted more influence.[9]

"There was considerable change caused by the overthrow of the
three House chairmen," says former Democratic Congressman Paul
Rogers of Florida. "The large freshman class in 1975 was very supportive of changes in seniority so they could have a greater say.
Probably forty new people were brought into the power structure
of the House, into the decision-making, and the power was spread.
The overthrow made chairmen much more solicitous of other
members of their committees, more willing to listen to other people. Also, the provision that the Caucus must approve chairmen

made them very conscious of the thinking of the entire Democratic group." Common Cause President Fred Wertheimer agrees: "There was a change in the way committee chairmen functioned. There's not the kind of arbitrariness in either the Senate or the House as existed before the overthrow in 1975."

## Seniority Changes in the Senate

The seniority system in the Senate never experienced a cataclysmic blow as it did in the House, and no Senate chairmen were ever set aside by a successful challenge. However, the mood in the Senate had changed also. Michael Pertschuk, counsel to the Senate Commerce Committee at the time the three House chairmen were removed (and later a vigorous chairman of the Federal Trade Commission), observed that it caused Senate chairmen to become sensitive to the possibility that their seniority could be disregarded. "To some extent," Pertschuk says, "it meant that the individual committee members had a stronger claim to fair treatment than they might have had before. It also limited the arbitrariness of the chairman, which was healthy. So, even though 1975 was the only year that chairmen were removed—and none was in the Senate—it changed things."

Charles Ferris, who served as counsel to the Senate Democratic Policy Committee in the 1960s and 1970s before being appointed chairman of the Federal Communications Commission, says that seniority was weakened by the greater turnover of members. "Seniority is predicated on much less turnover than they have now.[10] If the seniority system appears to be weaker, I think it's because the majority has no seniority. The system works best when there is an institutional memory. The loss of that memory is what changed the seniority system the most."

You will find very few people now running for office on the grounds that their seniority is a big asset to their districts.
                                                        —Congressman Barber Conable

## Notes

1. Roger H. Davidson, "Senate Leaders," in *Congress Reconsidered*, 3rd edition (Washington, D.C.: Congressional Quarterly, Inc., 1985), p. 226.

2. See Chapter 6.

3. Barbara Hinckley, *The Seniority System in Congress* (Bloomington: Indiana University Press, 1971).

4. *Congressional Record*, 84th Cong., 2d sess., 1956, S 3822.

5. John Bell Williams of Mississippi was dropped from the fifth position on the District of Columbia Committee and from the second on the Interstate Commerce Committee, thereby losing the chairmanship of the latter when Oren Harris retired in 1967. Refused reinstatement on Commerce by the Democratic Caucus in 1967, he campaigned for and was elected governor of Mississippi later that year. Freshman Congressman Albert W. Watson of South Carolina, kept at the bottom of the Post Office and Civil Service Committee, resigned from Congress, ran successfully as a Republican in a special election, and was assigned by his new party to the Interstate Commerce Committee.

6. Morse broke with the Republicans by announcing his support for Adlai Stevenson's presidential bid in October 1952. During the 83rd Congress, he called himself an "independent," but voted with the Democrats to organize the 84th Congress and formally joined the Democratic Party six weeks later. Strom Thurmond of South Carolina announced his support for Goldwater's presidential campaign and switched to the Republican Party in 1964.

7. Sizable opposition was registered against the following chairmen: Richard Ichord of Missouri, Internal Security Committee, 108–49; Wayne Hays of Ohio, Administration Committee, 117–39; William Poage of Texas, Agriculture Committee, 169–48; Chet Holifield of California, Government Operations Committee, 172–46; F. Edward Hebert of Louisiana, Armed Services, 154–41; and Wright Patman of Texas, Banking and Currency, 115–40. The least opposition was registered against Melvin Price of Illinois, Ethics Committee, 156–2.

8. See Chapter 7.

9. The average age of all House chairmen, if the three had not been defeated, would have been seventy-seven; the average age of the three new chairmen was fifty-nine.

10. See Thomas E. Mann and Norman Ornstein, *The New Congress* (Washington, D.C.: American Enterpise Institute for Public Policy Research, 1981), p. 33.

# 2

# What Is Congress
# and How Can It Work Better?

All legislative Powers herein granted shall be vested in a Congress
of the United States, which shall consist of a Senate and House of
Representatives.

—Constitution of the United States

The Congress of the United States is the representative branch of
our tripartite government, a bicameral legislature composed of a
100-member Senate and a 435-member House of Representatives.
But Congress is more than the institution that writes the laws that
govern our nation. Just what is Congress?

"What is Congress? Congress is the greatest show on earth, that's
what it is," says WETA Washington correspondent Paul Duke, who
covered the Hill during the 1960s and 1970s for the *Wall Street
Journal* and NBC News. "Congress is the most exciting place in
town. It's the greatest marketplace of democracy, and looking at it
through the eyes of a reporter, it's by far the most interesting and
exciting beat in Washington."

"Congress is a body that not only legislates; it also informs
the people, investigates, and oversees programs," says Senate
Minority Leader Robert C. Byrd of West Virginia. "To paraphrase
Franklin D. Roosevelt, 'If something were to happen to the Congress, if we no longer had a Congress, we would no longer have a
republic.' "

"Congress is the people's representatives," says Democratic
Senator Lawton Chiles of Florida. "The Founding Fathers knew

what they were talking about when they wanted a republic and a representative government rather than a truer sort of democracy."

"Congress is one of the world's greatest legislative bodies," says Democratic Congressman Morris Udall of Arizona, "although the special interests have a little too much to say—a little more than they should, and more than ordinary people—but I think Congress is a pretty good institution. It was never designed for efficiency or quick action; it was designed for checks and balances and to take its time and change national policy where needed carefully and slowly."

Former Democratic Congressman Frank Ikard of Texas defines Congress as "a group of people, representative of geographical areas of the country, who gather in an effort to enact the rules that cover our conduct and the conduct of our government." He says, however, that "there's a lot of confusion about it. Not many people understand we are a republic which means that, in my view at least, we are not a democracy where everybody votes on every issue. You vote for your representatives." Ikard laments that "we have become more and more of the opinion that we are a democracy, obsessed with polls and all that which has kind of reduced Congress to just a conduit of information. I think it was not originally conceived to be a body that would be popularly elected. The founders of our country were afraid of the House of Representatives because they didn't have much confidence in the people, contrary to all the Fourth of July speeches."

"Congress is *not* a group of leaders," says former Republican Congressman Barber Conable of New York, "and it's not a group of philosopher kings. It's a group that is carefully designed to try to give the people what they want. It does what is necessary, ultimately—and frequently, very late in the game. It's way behind the curve because of its accountability: it tends to be dragged kicking and screaming into recognizing change which may be pervasive elsewhere. This is because of our fear of getting out on any limbs." Conable regrets that "the people don't understand that. They want Congress to be efficient and to have leaders and philosopher-kings. We are not leaders; we are representatives. The Congress is not on the cutting edge of change. We reflect consensus and consensus means that everybody else knows about it before we do and everybody else has acted on it because they know they can't rely on government to be an efficient instrument of change. Government has to be dragged along kicking and screaming after the basic decision has been made by society as a whole."

## Does Congress Work?

Perhaps the most vital question that must be asked is: Does Congress work?

"You bet it does!" says Barber Conable. "Congress does what it was designed to do: give the people what they want. Members do this to assure reelection. Congress was designed to give the people what they want and do it only when we're sure we know what they want, not when we design what will be better for them. Wilbur Mills[1] pointed that out in a hearing when he told us that Edmund Burke, famous for saying, 'The people do not just want our votes, they want our judgment,' was defeated in the next election."

"Congress has always worked, though in a cumbersome, awkward way," says Paul Duke, "and sometimes the lawmakers are well behind public opinion. But I see no other way in a free society to really resolve our differences except through this method of representative government where there's a clash of ideas and viewpoints. Somehow out of all this churning maw you make slow progress in this country. It's even progress and sometimes unfair progress. Nonetheless there's no other way in a democracy that we can really effectively institute public policy except through this way of having the people's representatives make the decisions about what we do in this country. And it works."

"When Congress works and when it works best is in an absolute crisis," says Senator Chiles. "Congress has a very hard time—and this is not just Congress but democracy, so it goes further than that, I think—in trying to anticipate, in trying to make moves before there's a crisis. I think part of this is that we have lost our real verve for leadership. That, I think, is where Congress is getting worse and worse: fewer and fewer people are willing to stand up and lead. In the words of former Democratic Senator Herman Talmadge of Georgia, 'Don't ever try to fix a problem the people don't know they got.'"

"Congress is not efficient and frequently damage results from our slowness to recognize change," adds Barber Conable. "This doesn't mean that it isn't the best available mechanism for giving the people what they want because the purpose of Congress is not to be efficient but to ensure that the central government does not become efficient."

## Lengthen House Terms

How can Congress be made to work better? Of the many suggestions offered in recent years, lengthening the term of House members from the present two years (which the Founding Fathers believed would ensure a close relationship between Congressmen and their constituents) to four is perhaps the most frequently mentioned. Haynes Johnson of the *Washington Post* agrees that "it makes a lot of sense to have a four-year term for Congressmen" because running every two years "forces them to return to their districts every weekend. They're literally running for reelection the minute they're elected. I just think you can't deal with the intricacies of the issues and master them if you run back to the Rotary parade or the rodeo function in your hometown every weekend, and that's what they're forced to do. That doesn't make much sense to me. So, a four-year term would free them, at least for a large part of that time, to work in Congress."

Alan Boyd, who served as President Lyndon B. Johnson's Transportation Secretary, would establish four-year terms for the House. He says that more time between campaigns would alleviate the "merry-go-round" of Washington-based constituent meetings, committee meetings, and debates followed by "running home to politic and protect your rear against the opportunists which each representative was before he or she got elected. It's just a dog's life."

## Revise the Senate Cloture Rule

Former Democratic Senator Eugene McCarthy of Minnesota lists five major changes he would like to see instituted. First, a return to the 1946 rules pertaining to the number of committees and sub-committees;[2] second, abolition of the codes of ethics "which are ludicrous"; third, elimination of the Federal Election Law; fourth, repeal of the Budget Act; fifth, a change in the filibuster rule "because today you don't have an honest filibuster anymore. They are filibustering by amendment and procedure. The old filibuster was a 'trial by ordeal,' almost like a duel. You laid you body on the line and the question was whether or not you could stand it physically. It was a gentlemen's showdown, but now it's just technique and monkey business."

Most congressional observers agree with McCarthy on changing the cloture (filibuster) rule in the Senate.[3] Cloture is instituted when three-fifths (formerly two-thirds) of the Senate votes to end debate. "The cloture procedure still isn't adequate," says former Democratic Senator William Hathaway of Maine, "but it's better than it used to be. It still has a long way to go before it's improved to the point where it makes legislation run along a lot smoother."

William Hathaway cites Democratic Senator John Melcher of Montana's filibustering for two days at the close of the first session of the 98th Congress as an example of how the Senate can be tied up by one man: "The vote was 85 to 5 in favor of cloture, and that was just on *bringing up* the natural gas bill. One person can delay legislation and even kill it if it is brought up toward the end of a session. That certainly isn't what we conceive as a good practice in a democratic form of government. The post-cloture rules must be changed because a lot of good legislation is stalled, and even killed, that way. Members should have a chance to vote on legislation. The alternative problem is that there could be the tyranny of the majority, which there is to an extent in the House because the House can vote to cut off all debate after a certain length of time. So, an element of the tyranny of the majority is there and I certainly wouldn't want to see that in the Senate."

He proposes adopting "a simple rule that would cut off debate after it has been going on for an hour if supported by two-thirds of the Senate. That would eliminate having to file a cloture petition then wait the couple of days and the one hundred hours allowed after cloture has been invoked. The way it stands now is kind of ridiculous."

Former Democratic Senator Gale McGee of Wyoming, although not totally opposed to the filibuster rule, agrees that it must be changed because of "the way it is being used." He would limit post-cloture filibuster "very dramatically," and suggests changing

Senate rules to make it "acceptable to perform the service that is legitimate for the filibuster. We must stop the nonsense of allowing just one Senator to stop anything he wants to stop at any given time."

"All of us have seen legislation carefully constructed at the committee level, reported out of the committee, perhaps unanimously, discussed and debated thoroughly on the floor—yet not voted on," says Anthony Zagami, counsel to the Joint Committee on Printing. "This could be legislation that would be passed 90 to 10, that is, if it were voted on. Yet, that legislation sometimes will disappear simply because the rules in the Senate allow for a filibuster and many procedural delays. I would like to see something closer to the House rules where debate is limited on all legislation and their Rules Committee exercises some degree of control over the scheduling of legislation and the time that may be spent on each bill. Much of the Senate's time is spent on dealing with procedural matters, time that could be better spent if they were truly dealing with the legislation at hand."

"The filibuster becomes ridiculous when it's used for relatively minor purposes endlessly," says former Democratic Senator Gaylord Nelson of Wisconsin. "Historically the idea was that nothing important should be stampeded through the Senate if one-third—now it's two-fifths—thought it was a bad idea. The filibuster allowed that group to hold up the legislation." Nelson outlined the recent "post-cloture filibuster," which he considers abusive, and which was frequently used by the late Democratic Senator James A. Allen of Alabama. After cloture was invoked, and each Senator was permitted but one hour to speak on the bill involved, "Jim Allen would print 300 amendments, bring up each one of them without discussion, and call for a roll call. He would use only ten seconds of his time while tying up the Senate for the fifteen or twenty minutes it takes to complete a roll call. Then he would call up another one. So Allen, with his 300 amendments, could take two weeks using up his one hour. That was never intended, and this nonsense should be stopped." As a result, Nelson adds, "the threat of a filibuster causes all kinds of problems. It has become a device by which one person can hold up the whole Senate and you cannot get to a vote. If everyone had to stand up and use his or her one hour speaking, without using devices, the damned thing would be disposed of reasonably and 'filibuster by amendment' would be impossible."

Former Democratic Senator James O. Abourezk of South Dakota says that "the power of the filibuster allows any member to hold up legislation through the use of Senate rules. If a Senator knows how to use those rules he can acquire some degree of influence and power." Abourezk tells how that became clear to him late in his career: "I though it was quite funny that even after I had announced my retirement, Senators used to come to me and say, 'Is it okay if I introduce this legislation?' They would ask me because I had conducted a quite successful filibuster and they thought I might try to block their legislation if they didn't clear it with me first. I couldn't have cared less, but it was funny."

Charles Ferris suggests "changing the rules on the filibuster so that the majority can work its will when cloture is invoked. This should be an orderly procedure." He agrees that Senator Allen's "filibuster by amendment" procedure should be prevented in the future. "Once the overwhelming majority has worked its will, you should say, 'All right.' When cloture is invoked, the minority then must accept the fact that its objections have been listened to. However strongly you may feel, the system has to work, and that must be accepted."

Samuel Shaffer, chief congressional correspondent for *Newsweek* for thirty years, would not change the filibuster rule fundamentally, but he would modify it to prevent abuses of the cloture system. Shaffer thinks that the loopholes in the rule should be "plugged," but he would not weaken the cloture rule itself. "Once sixty Senators want debate cut off, it should be done. It's not easy to get sixty Senators because the Senate believes it's the last arena in the world of free and unlimited debate, and the Senate wants to be a place where they can stand up against a current wave of hysteria and say, 'No, let's consider this further; let's think about it; let's debate it.' They are quite reluctant to cut off debate. So when there are sixty Senators—three-fifths—agreeing to cut off debate, then that debate should be cut off so the cloture petition cannot be frustrated."

The Senate Study Group's Pearson–Ribicoff Report[4] states that "too often amendments have been submitted solely for the purpose of delaying final action on the pending business on which cloture has been invoked. . . . [Because] there is no limit to the number of amendments that each Senator may call up . . . a single Senator may contrive to use much or more of the 100 hours with little or no accomplishment by calling up amendments and getting roll call votes on which it was evident to begin that there would not be agreement. . . . " The report recommends that "certain restrictions should be placed in the rule which would certainly aid in shortening, if not eliminating, much of the post-cloture filibuster." While the Pearson–Ribicoff recommendations received praise from the Senate leadership and others, to date no action has been taken on modifying the filibuster rule.

## Money in Politics

Money, "the mother's milk of politics," is widely blamed for its influence on Congress.[5] Though not affecting the rules of the Congress directly, money or the lack of it has become increasingly important in the elective process. Most recommendations for reform call for changing or eliminating Political Action Committees (PACs) and instituting a system whereby members receive much of their financing through the national political parties.[6]

"The most critical change that needs to be made is in the means of financing elections," says former Congressman Paul Rogers. "I'm not sure which other mechanism will begin to cut the ties with the special interests that can raise the money and assert influence. They're [the Congress] going to have to work out some means of reducing spending. However, I'm not sure they will ever reduce the spending on elections unless every radio and television station gives so much time to each candidate, and, in addition, limits are set on how much can be spent." Rogers proposes a "blue-ribbon national commission because we're fast approaching what could become a national scandal about the way money now can be used to assert influence in the elective and the legislative process."

"The PAC system must be revised," says Tracy Mullin, former aide to Senate Minority Leader Hugh Scott. "It's a system that allows people to raise money and then keep it if they don't run, or build up a war chest, as much as they want, then retire with one million dollars unspent—it's theirs! That's crazy and insane, and as long as that continues, the system doesn't make any sense because the votes don't make any sense." However, Mullin feels that "there's more honesty in the Congress today because there are more reports to file and more public scrutiny. The days of people buying votes illegally are gone, replaced by the PAC system."

Democratic Senator William Proxmire of Wisconsin wants "some diminution—though I don't know how you would achieve it—of the power of money in politics. I can see what the ultimate goal ought to be, but how to get there is the question. What should be done is after a Senator has been elected once, or at the most twice, is to prohibit him from spending any money in his campaign at all. It would he hard to get this through the Senate, but it's what I've done in the last two elections. I spent $177 in my 1976 election, and $145 last time [1982]. The incumbent has an advantage: a newsletter, staff, all kinds of things an opponent doesn't have. It's unbalanced the way it is now, and I think the influence of money is very, very perverse. It's a tragedy that the forces that are organized have money. They may be right and they may be wrong, but they'll almost always prevail because they have that advantage. I think that's unfortunate."

"First of all you have to start with the money," agrees Haynes Johnson, "because as long as the single-issue groups and the PACs have the power they have—and the power is increasing in their ability to define and order legislation—it poses a dangerous prospect for the country. You start with the money, start with breaking up that possibility of power. That is the first and, it seems to me, the most obvious, recommendation."

"If Congress is to regain credibility—and that's terribly important if our system of government is to be preserved—it really must do something about campaign financing," said the late Democratic Senator Frank Church of Idaho. "Some way must be found to reimpose reasonable limits on what may be spent on campaigns, and that's not an easy task." Church said that when he first ran for the Senate in 1956, the general election campaign in Idaho cost $45,000; in contrast, he spent just under $2 million in 1980, and he was outspent two-to-one. "The amount of money that poured into Idaho," he said,"to 'auction off' that Senate seat came to about $10 a vote. Now, that's obscene!"

Senator Byrd agrees that "it costs a lot more money to run for the Senate than it did when I first came in. When I first ran for the Senate in 1958, both my senior colleague, Jennings Randolph, and I were able to campaign on a combined treasury of less than $50,000. Today a campaign costs a great deal more and one reason for that is that we are now in an age when candidates out of necessity must engage in a lot of television advertising. This is quite different from the way it was twenty-six years ago when I came to the Senate."

## Streamlining Congressional Procedure

There are numerous recommendations that would modify House and Senate procedures by decreasing the number of roll call votes, restructuring congressional sessions, and eliminating the current practice of writing legislation on the floor. Most frequently cited as a possible improvement is limiting the number of roll call votes. "I think endless roll call votes are terrible," says William Hathaway, "and I don't know what you're going to do about it."

Republican Senator James McClure of Idaho thinks that "organizing our time is the toughest thing we have to do in the Senate and we do it very poorly. I'd like to see the Congress in session Monday morning through Friday night three weeks of the month, and allow the fourth week to be spent doing the things that are now done on Mondays and Fridays. The 'Tuesday–Thursday club' just kills me. I'm not accusing people in the Congress of being lazy—far from it. They don't stay very long if they are. But if we are in [session] five days a week, three weeks a month, we wouldn't have to worry about whether or not 'this is the Monday or the Friday that we're going to have something important to do?' This is particularly true for those of us who are more than an hour and a half from Washington. I just think we could get an awful lot more done if we managed our time on a predictable basis so we could schedule our activities."

Republican Senator Barry Goldwater of Arizona complained recently on the Senate floor that "we sit around here day after day after day and never do a doggone thing. . . . This place is getting to be like a cookie farm."[7]

Former Senate Majority Leader Howard Baker of Tennessee proposed six-month long sessions "to restore Congress to its original and intended character as a citizen legislature." In April 1984, Senator Baker wrote that "Congress should be in session for only six or so months of the year—with four months at the beginning of the year devoted to the authorization process [enacting laws authorizing government action on matters of national importance] and two months in the fall devoted to the appropriation process [deciding how much the government should spend on those actions]. The other half of the year should be spent, not in Washington but in the rest of the country—seeing firsthand the practical effect of federal laws on private lives and enterprise, staying in personal touch with the people we're elected to represent, experiencing real life in America, not as distant observers, but as involved participants."[8]

Democratic Senator Dale Bumpers of Arkansas, on the other hand, says that Senator McClure's three-weeks-in-and-one-week-out proposal "is better than Senator Baker's suggestion of six months in session and six months out. It [Senator Baker's proposal] still wouldn't preclude a Senator from going home on any other weekend, particularly early in the session; it would simply bring some organization to it. Another possibility would be to make Mondays, Wednesdays, and Fridays legislative days, and have Tuesdays and Thursdays as committee days. That might make a lot of sense."

Former Senate Minority Leader Hugh Scott of Pennsylvania says "there's merit in Senator Baker's proposal that the Congress meet for a short time each year. Our sessions have been so cut up by the addition of so-called work periods at home—which used to be called vacations—that the actual number of days spent could be compressed into half a year, barring emergencies. There could be a provision that a session of Congress shall last for such and such a number of months, perhaps, and could be extended only by a two-thirds vote of each house or by call of the President." Scott recalls that when he was in the Senate "we used to add to the resolution at the end of each session that we could be called back 'upon the call of the Majority or the Minority Leader.' [Senate Majority Leader Mike] Mansfield and I had the right to call the Senate back into session, and we often wondered why someone didn't pick that up and kick about it."

Former Senator Hathaway also supports Senator Baker's suggestion of a six-month session because "members would better serve the public if they actually went home and lived with their constituents at least half of the year. Just going home every weekend and talking to the local service club and listening to their questions doesn't really give you a feel for what's going on back home. However, if you were home bumping into constituents day in and day out, you'd really find out a lot more about what they're thinking, what the real problems are. There's no reason why the legislative calendar couldn't be compacted into a six-month period. As we have it now, the Congress starts in January; yet not much of anything happens until the first of March. They're getting committee assignments, then there's the Lincoln Day recess, and this, that, and the other thing. Members of Congress are no different than anyone else: they'll put off everything until the last minute if they can. So you might as well just tell them that everything has got to be out of the way by the first of July."

Senator Proxmire challenged Senator Baker's proposal on the floor. "I think Baker is just plain wrong," Proxmire says. "It's ridiculous to argue that Senators can work half time now, spending the other half at home, as he says, 'earning a living.' That sounds all right, but what kind of jobs will they get? You know what they'd get? They would be hired by the biggest industry that could afford it. If they returned to a law firm, they'd be retained by the big steel company, the big bank, and so forth. The average constituent who doesn't have any kind of financial capability or power would have much less influence than he has now. . . . I think you would have a much less effective democracy. Furthermore, I don't think you would represent people as well."

Senator Bumpers would limit the hours each day the Senate spends in debate, "cutting it down very dramatically. I would provide, for example, that we go into session at four in the afternoon and the Majority Leader would decide that a certain bill is to be voted on at, say, ten the next night. The rules would have to be revised but there should be certain limitations so we wouldn't make a dictator out of the Majority Leader. I would also suggest logging the time that Senators were on the floor. That would become important, not how many votes you cast, but how much time you were on the floor listening to debate. Then I would cut debate time down so we would not have to listen to some Senator droning on for thirty minutes with a text that he doesn't even understand, let alone the other Senators understanding it."

Senator Bumpers would set up "sort of a time clock system. Since no Senator wants to go into his next election saying he voted less than 90 percent of the roll calls—I would limit the time on bills very specifically and also provide a new criterion, similar to voting attendance: sitting attendance. I'm not sure how you would do it, maybe just hand them a time clock, but if you're not in your seat, then the next time you ran for reelection that would be publicized rather than your voting percentage."

Former Senator Gaylord Nelson adds that "if amendments offered on the floor are substantive, they should be sent back to committee and hearings held. There must be more discipline, a dramatic reduction in the consideration of proposals that come off the tops of our heads and are offered as amendments on the floor. It's a massive, tough question, and nobody is seriously addressing it now."

Former Senator Baker suggested incorporating a five-year "sunset" provision into basic laws which would mean that a law would expire automatically unless legislation were enacted for its continuance. Theoretically, less legislation would be introduced if it were certain to be reviewed for effectiveness in five years. Further, there would be some predictability in the congressional agenda. "Such an approach would allow Congress to examine how the bureaucracy has interpreted the law in its rules and regulations; to see whether or not the law is having its intended effect, and to determine whether it should be renewed, revised, or removed," wrote Senator Baker in the *New York Times Magazine*, April 1, 1984. Haynes Johnson, although he does not speak to the "sunset" proposal, recommends that Congress prepare its agenda in advance, the leaders of both parties determining the schedule of hearings, and "be ruthless in cutting out filibusters and the 2:00 A.M. roll call votes. It's not quite as democratic," he says, "but it seems to me it's better in the end for democracy."

Congress is not only one of the world's great legislative bodies. It's also a good reflection of the American people.
—Congressman Morris Udall

## Notes

1. Former chairman of the House Ways and Means Committee.
2. The Legislative Reorganization Act of 1946, among other changes, reduced the number of standing committees in the Senate from thirty-

three to fifteen and in the House from forty-eight to nineteen, and more strictly defined committee jurisdictions.

3. See Raymond E. Wolfinger, "Filibusters' Majority Rule, Presidential Leadership, and Senate Norms," in *Congressional Behavior*, ed. Nelson Polsby (New York: Random House, 1970), p. 111.

4. The Senate Study Group, headed by former Senators James A. Pearson (R., Kansas) and Abraham I. Ribicoff (D., Connecticut), was established by the Senate leadership to make recommendations on Senate practices and procedure. It issued its report in April 1983 but no action has been taken on its proposals.

5. See T. R. Reid, *Congressional Odyssey* (San Francisco: W. H. Freeman & Company, 1980).

6. See Gary C. Jacoban, "Parties and PACs in Congressional Elections," in *Congress Reconsidered*, pp. 131–156.

7. *Congressional Record*, June 12, 1984, 98th Congress; 2d sess., S 6974.

8. *The New York Times Magazine*, April 1, 1984.

# 3

# A Look at the Seniority System

I feel about seniority the way that Churchill did about democracy: it is the worst of all systems except for the others.
                                    —Hugh Scott, former Senate Minority Leader

The great thing about seniority is that it's the least worst of all the systems that you might use here.
                                    —Senator William Proxmire

That it is the "least worst of all systems," in the words of Senator Proxmire, is the most compelling argument given by seniority's supporters. Although they recognize that other methods may reward ability, competence, or even brilliance, only seniority is nondiscriminatory and automatically precludes the internecine fighting so disruptive to the legislative process.

"And it works!" said the late Frank Church, reflecting on his Senate career of more than a quarter century. "One thing that can be said about seniority, among all the arguments pro and con, is that it works. It is a definite, understandable, unambiguous way to determine who gets what position in each committee as well as who gets which assignments. It eliminates all the warfare and the political jockeying for position that otherwise would go on in Congress."

"I see no substitute for the seniority system, and I say that based on thirty years of coverage of both houses of Congress," says Samuel Shaffer. "It has worked out better than any other system, because to run an unruly body of four hundred thirty-five House members or one hundred Senators, there must be some form of discipline. Eliminating the seniority system would produce chaos in the Congress."

Strong supporters of the seniority system, however, do admit that it has shortcomings. Former Republican Senator Robert Taft, Jr., of Ohio says: "It tends to keep people in slots and can be wasteful in that it doesn't use the best abilities of those serving in the first few years in the Congress. However, it's hard to come up with satisfactory alternatives."

"The seniority system has some shortcomings," agrees Democratic Senator Quentin Burdick of North Dakota, "but particularly when you are dealing with the day-to-day problems in the Senate I don't know what you would supplant it with. I have questions about the seniority system, but I haven't heard anybody advocate a better alternative. How would you manage the show without a system like this? That's the first question I like to ask anyone who's in opposition to the present system, and until I get alternatives suggested, I don't know how else you would run it. For instance, how would you assign Senate offices? It's a simple little matter, but how would you do it? Put all the names in a hat and draw every year? If a new Senator came in, you'd have to have another drawing from the fish bowl. I think it would be very disorderly."

"There would be total chaos without the seniority system" agrees Charles Ferris, who has worked in both the legislative and executive branches. "Years ago when Senate chairmen were elected by all the Senators, many times they could not coalesce into a majority and there would be a standoff. Sometimes it took a hundred ballots to elect the chairman of one committee. You'd be spending all your time organizing if every position were going to be decided that way. Seniority is a very orderly system."

"Without the seniority system," says Patrick O'Donnell, who served as a congressional lobbyist for Presidents Nixon and Ford, "there would be too much competition among members striving to be leaders and running for congressional office, in addition to running for reelection. I like the seniority system because I don't think there's anything much better."

However, as Senator Byrd points out, the seniority system has two sides. "The down side," Byrd explains, "is that from time to time a more able Senator may have to give way to another Senator with greater seniority in an area where the more able Senator would have more expertise. And, as a usual thing, as the years come and go, a member gains in expertise and knowledge of the subject matter that comes before a subcommittee or committee of which he's chairman. From that standpoint, it can usually produce a chairman or ranking member who has the longest experience in dealing with a particular subject. By virtue of that experience he has gained a tremendous amount of expertise and knowledge in that field."

"There is a certain fairness about seniority," points out Senator Chiles. "Whether you're black, white, or yellow, come from the south or the north, based on the time you go on the committee, you come up the ladder and pick up experience along the way. Seniority has some real handicaps, one of them being that you almost have to be on one committee so long before you get a chance to get into the saddle that you may be past your best days. But, at the same time, there are drawbacks on any other way that you could do it because if there were an outright election, we could have a palace coupe every six months."

"All ongoing organizations must have some system of establishing leadership," says former Congressman William R. Poage of Texas, "and from earliest times man has used seniority. The elders have been leaders in the family, in the church, in the village, and in many forms of government. Modern labor unions rely on seniority to control opportunity for advancement. In Congress it's especially desirable to reduce the opportunity for personal advancement which would result in lasting ill feeling. Without the seniority system, every member is invited to undermine his committee chairman in order to secure an advantageous position for himself."

"Seniority may not be the best, but it sure as hell is better than whatever the alternatives are," says Washington lobbyist Tom C. Korologos, former Nixon White House lobbyist and former aide to Senator Wallace Bennett (R., Utah). "The alternatives involve logrolling for committee assignments, selling out, and buying votes to get the chairmanship. That's not the way it should work. I'm for the seniority system one hundred percent unless you come up with something better. And the alternatives are not any good at all."

"I think among all the alternatives available or that have been dreamed of," says former Senator Gale McGee, "the seniority system is the most rational approach to orderliness; otherwise, there is buying tradeoffs, trading behind backs, and all those things. The seniority system avoids that sort of skullduggery; secondly, year in and year out, it produces someone with experience. Thus, seniority gives a sense of perspective or a sense of history at the helm. I think those are irreplaceable by any other method."

"It doesn't make for a congenial atmosphere when the chairman looks around and discovers that everybody around him has a knife out ready to cut a deal or cut his throat."says Washington lobbyist Maurice Rosenblatt. "You have to keep playing politics or you no longer will be chairman. There's something to authority having a certain continuity."

"I haven't heard a suggestion for a more workable system,"says former Senator Gaylord Nelson. "The question that must be asked is: 'What is the alternative to the seniority system?' I don't know just how you would design one without creating a great deal of divisiveness. If there are any alternatives, I don't know what the system might be."

"There's more to be said for seniority than to be said against it," says former Senator Eugene McCarthy. "My experience was that seniority generally gave order and was a good way to proceed. Members of Congress can develop a very high level of frustration and the prospect of becoming a committee chairman can, in many cases, reduce these feelings of frustration. Seniority gives stability to Congress, especially in the House where there is need for more discipline and continuity because of the nature of its membership and organization."

"A system which ignores seniority lends itself to favoritism and to pandering to vanity and finding weaknesses in one's colleagues to secure the position of chairman,"says former Senate Minority Leader Hugh Scott. "The advantage of the seniority system is that it recognizes, too, that people should have some right to plan their future and to expect that with the passage of time they would be given more responsibility. It sometimes works badly; but, in the vast majority of cases, it really works."

"If there were not seniority," points out Senator Prox-mire,"there would be all kinds of politicking and maneuvering to see who's going to be chairman of this committee or that committee, and there would be backbiting and all sorts of problems. They say you should select on the basis of excellence and competence, but how do you determine that? Everyody thinks he's good or he wouldn't be in the Senate. So I think seniority is probably a way of avoiding all kinds of difficulties and at least it does have an objective determination of who has the experience and who has been on the committee for longer than the others have."

## Safe Districts and One-Party States

Seniority, because it rewards length of service, benefits members of Congress who come from "safe" districts or states and thus are continually reelected. "The only people who survive under the seniority system are those who have one-party constituencies," says Maurice Rosenblatt. "You're not likely to get somebody from an area where you have vital contests, and areas where you do have vital contests give you the most talented people. They have to be. For example, the border states where there are challenges and contests and swings, such as Maryland and New Jersey, elect people who must be much more alert. They cannot settle back but must remain open to challenge. They become versatile—and versatility is terribly important in the Congress where they deal with so many issues."

The members who are reelected again and again by comfortable majorities are blessed with districts or states that have a stayed and steady population. These members (see Table 1) are the ones who do so much to create the institutional memory.[1] To some observers only a safe constituency can produce the best legislators. "If a person rises to power just because he comes from a safe district, that's fine with me," says Tom Korologos. "The longer a guy stays the better. A safe district is created by the man who votes his constituents' views. On the other hand, there were many Senators who were good guys, nice guys, who forgot the folks back home who sent them." Korologos recalls the time that former Senator Gale McGee was speaking to a group of his constituents in Casper, Wyoming. "Gale was bragging that he was a member of the Senate Foreign Relations Committee and had been to over one hundred different countries. 'Well Gale,' an old cowboy asked the Senator, 'why don't you come out and see *us* once in a while?'" Korologos concludes that "the political graveyards in this town are filled with great brilliant statesmen who didn't follow the views of the folks back home."

**Table 1**
**The Twenty-Five Longest Serving Members of Congress**

| | |
|---|---|
| Rep. and Sen. Carl Hayden (D., Arizona) | 57 years |
| Rep. Carl Vinson (D., Georgia) | 50 years |
| Rep. Emmanuel Celler (D., New York) | 50 years |
| Rep. Sam Rayburn (D., Texas) | 49 years |
| Rep. Wright Patman (D., Texas) | 47 years |
| Rep. Joseph Cannon (R., Illinois) | 46 years |
| Rep. Adolph Sabath (D., Illinois) | 46 years |
| Rep. and Sen. Lister Hill (D., Alabama) | 45 years |
| Rep. George Mahon (D., Texas) | 44 years |
| Rep. and Sen. Warren Magnuson (D., Washington) | 44 years |
| Rep. and Sen. Justin Morrill (R., Vermont) | 44 years |
| Rep. and Sen. William Allison (R., Iowa) | 43 years |
| Rep. and Sen. Henry Jackson (D., Washington) | 43 years |
| Rep. and Sen. Carter Glass (D., Virginia) | 42 years |
| Rep. Jamie Whitten (D., Mississippi) | 42 years |
| Rep. and Sen. John Sparkman (D., Alabama) | 42 years |
| Rep. W. R. Poage (D., Texas) | 42 years |
| Rep. Robert Doughton (D., North Carolina) | 42 years |
| Rep. Joseph Martin (R., Massachusetts) | 42 years |
| Rep. Clarence Cannon (D., Missouri) | 41 years |
| Rep. and Sen. Kenneth McKellar (D., Tennessee) | 41 years |
| Rep. and Sen. William Frye (R., Maine) | 40 years |
| Rep. and Sen. Carl Curtis (R., Nebraska) | 40 years |
| Rep. Leslie Arends (R., Illinois) | 40 years |
| Rep. and Sen. Eugene Hale (R., Maine) | 40 years |

"A safe district," agrees Samuel Shaffer, "allows a chairman to exercise his judgment even when it might conflict with the majority opinion in his district or state. A committee chairman has to be someone who can take gambles against the immediate buffets of change, and a safe district allows this. A good example would be former House Rules Chairman Republican Leo Allen of Galena, Illinois. During the 80th Congress there was a big demand for universal military service, and so strongly had national sentiment been whipped up that it looked as if legislation to enact it would be unstoppable. The leaders of the House of Representatives knew that universal military service would be unwise and they wanted to stop the legislation. So House Speaker Joe Martin asked Leo Allen not to clear the bill through the Rules Committee.[2] It was only because Allen came from a safe district that he could feel free to refuse to take the bill up. And the national demand soon dissipated, never to surface again."

"The test of a member of the House or Senate is whether his people reelect him," says former Republican Congressman Melvin R. Laird of Wisconsin, who also served as Secretary of Defense. "The more they reelect him, the more you can rely on that particular person. People make the right judgments in elections, so a man who has had many terms has proved himself with his people, and that's the important thing. While you can win a popularity contest with your colleagues—and that may be important—it isn't as important as winning back home. That's the true test of a politician. Committee chairmen are good people and they accumulate their seniority because they are good Representatives and good Senators."

## Autocratic Chairmen

Safe districts and repeated reelection may produce excellent statesmen, but the power bestowed on committee chairmen can sometimes allow and even encourage abuses. "Every aspect of Congress's work is affected by a rigid, unbending, all-pervasive seniority system which gives a few men great national power with no national responsibility and selects key congressional leaders on a basis which excludes any consideration of ability," wrote Congressman Morris Udall twenty years ago. "The committee member who—regardless of ability—has served twenty years is not just 5 percent more powerful than the member who has served nineteen years. If the former is chairman of a committee he is *100 percent* more powerful."

"Ten, twenty years ago a tiny, tiny handful of men controlled virtually everything in the House and Senate," says Frank Silbey, who served as an investigator for committees in both houses. "Committee chairmen were uncrowned kings, they were barons, they presided over their own domains. The lines of authority were clearly defined and you violated them or sought to circumvent them at your peril."

"There was far too much power exercised by the chairmen of the major committees," says ABC newsman Bob Clark. "A chairman could be quite ruthless in holding down younger, more liberal, members or just members he disagreed with."

Most of these powerful chairmen were from one-party states or districts, Southerners, and conservatives. "House Rules committee Chairman Judge Howard Smith of Virginia was not only conservative, he was reactionary," says Shaffer. "He would delay civil rights bills that would come to the Rules Committee from the Judiciary Committee where the request would be made to send them to the floor. Howard Smith would absent himself, denying even the Speaker. He would disappear for days at a time, saying 'Well, I was busy painting my barn.' " Rosenblatt agrees that Judge Smith "ran his committee as a private barony. If he didn't like legislation he would just go to his farm and disappear, and that bill would be bottled up until finally it was withdrawn. Later there were attempts to pack the Rules Committee with members who would be more amenable to bending to the will of the House, but when Judge Smith was head of the Rules Committee, if he didn't like a bill and did not think it was good, it didn't get on the schedule."

Former House Rules Committee Chairman Richard Bolling of Missouri talked about the committee's power in the late 1930s: "Right after Franklin Roosevelt's great victory and our incredible [Democratic] majority of three to one in the House—there were fewer than one hundred Republicans in 1937—the Rules Committee fell into the hands of the conservative coalition. Everything concentrated within the Rules Committee, and that's where the conservative coalition had its strength. But, in those days no one would talk about the conservative coalition, and that included the media."

Another powerful Southern chairman was Democrat Carl Vinson of Georgia who headed the House Armed Services Committee. "A terrible autocrat," according to Maurice Rosenblatt. "Vinson treated

the U.S. Navy as if it were his toy boat in his bathtub. If you were
a freshman on his committee, you got to ask one question—that is,
if the committee hadn't adjourned and the hearing was still in progress and the witness was not exhausted. In your second term, you
got to ask two questions, and in your third term, you got three
questions." Former Senator Scott agrees that Vinson was "an example of an autocratic chairman who would not permit newcomers
to take part in the proceedings at all. If a new member volun-
teered, he was immediately gaveled down and put in his place."
Samuel Shaffer recalls that Vinson was "one of the shrewdest politicians and infighters in the history of the House of Representatives. He ran his committee like a one-man show, yet he was smart
enough to know when he should change course. Actually his powers were not resented and the members stood in awe of him."

Vinson's power extended even to choosing his successor, accomplished in a fashion that, it could be said, both maintained and
breached seniority. Melvin Laird recounts: "When Vinson was
leaving Congress he wanted Mendel Rivers of South Carolina to
succeed him as chairman. However, there were two people between Rivers and Vinson, Representatives Paul J. Kilday and
Overton Brooks. Vinson had House Speaker John McCormack move
Brooks to McCormack's place as chairman of the Science and Space
Committee, which removed him from the Armed Services Committee, and together McCormack and Vinson got Paul Kilday appointed to the Military Court of Justice. Then Mendel Rivers moved
up to chairman."

F. Edward Hebert of Louisiana, chairman of the House Armed
Services Committee, was another Southern chairman who, according to Shaffer, "made his committee almost a one-man show which
was very frustrating to the other members." Rosenblatt agrees that
"Hebert was atrocious. He talked to Congresswoman Pat Schroe-
der who was on his committee in a horrible way. He was vulgar
and crude."

Otto Passman of Louisiana, chairman of a House Appropriations
subcommittee on Foreign Affairs, was "either drunk with power or
senile or both," recalls Shaffer, "and quite often he would hold up
or threaten to cut a foreign aid bill unless he had his way on some
project in his district." However, Shaffer points out, "there are
ways around this obstructionism: the President of the United States

spoke to the Speaker of the House who then conferred with George Mahon of Texas, chairman of the House Appropriations Committee, who used his powers as chairman to pack Passman's subcommittee so he would not have a majority of votes. The foreign aid bill came through."

On the Senate side, Judiciary Chairman James O. Eastland of Mississippi "totally controlled all legislation handled by his committee," recalls Dr. Floyd Riddick, Senate Parliamentarian Emeritus. "No bill emerged that he did not support and each Judiciary Committee bill was passed in his version—intact—on the floor." Charles Ferris points out that Senator Eastland killed 128 civil rights bills in his committee during the 1950s and the early 1960s. "They were introduced, and that was the end of it. That was the graveyard, and he admitted it," Ferris says.

"The seniority system did give us some chairmen who, because of their longevity, were not very good," says Paul Duke. "But, on the other hand, the situation wasn't as bad as it was frequently depicted. The truth is that there is no perfect way to choose a committee chairman, and I have modified my views over the years and now conclude that the seniority sytem is not as bad as many have said."

## Aging Chairmen

That seniority allows, and even creates, autocratic and dictatorial chairmen is the most frequent criticism of the system. But, its detractors also charge that the seniority system can and has led to chairmanships held by members of Congress far beyond their prime. Senator Bumpers says that "sometimes the aging process itself works against a particular member: the longer he stays here the less crisp his mind is, and yet the more powerful he becomes. To allow some person to continue up the seniority ladder and hold positions of great power and responsibility in this country when he has indicated time and time again that he has no appreciation for history and has very little qualification for the position he holds is a bad system."

Samuel Shaffer cites the late Senator Kenneth McKellar of Tennessee, chairman of Senate Appropriations, as "so senile that committee business had become a shambles. A Cabinet officer would

appear before the committee to justify the budget for his department and McKellar would start cross-examining him and fall asleep.
The witness would continue talking because it would have been
rude to point out that the chairman was asleep. Then McKellar
would wake up with a start and say, 'Why didn't you answer my
question?' when the man had been answering the question for fifteen or twenty minutes."

Democratic Senator Theodore Francis Green of Rhode Island
remained as chairman of the Senate Foreign Relations Committee
until he was ninety-one and Senate Democrats finally persuaded
him to step aside in favor of William Fulbright of Arkansas. "That's
a pretty high old age to be an active chairman of a committee,"
reflects Hugh Scott.

However, not all elderly chairmen are active. George Herman
of CBS remembers that Senator Carl Hayden of Arizona "was in
his eighties and his attention seemed to wander. Sometimes you
thought he was asleep."

"The only change I would make in seniority,"says Frank Ikard,"is
that I would cut it off at the age of seventy-five or something where
a person couldn't be chairman of a committee beyond that age, but
he would serve as a 'chairman emeritus' or some sort of position
with status that would give him some influence."

"Who's to say when someone is too old?" asks John McConnell,
who served as top aide to Senate Majority Whip Russell Long.
"Some are old at sixty; others are vigorous at eighty. The democratic process is in question. Who can tell constituents of a state
or a district who should represent them?"

Ineffectual chairmen are not always senile, Eugene McCarthy
points out: "My first committee, the House Post Office and Civil
Service Committee, was chaired by Thomas Murray of Texas who
had a drinking problem. About every six weeks or so he would hit
it pretty hard to the point that he would disappear for a week. We
passed a rule that we would meet every other Thursday whether
the chairman was there or not. This meant that about every fourth
or fifth Thursday he was missing, and we could pass most of the
legislation we had been working on. Murray, who was quite com-
mitted to his office, would always come back and act as chairman,
handling the legislation which had been passed over his objections."

Many powerful, even arbitrary, chairmen are highly respected, their influence based on solid knowledge of history, parliamentary skills, and command of the intricacies of congressional procedure. Democratic Senator Richard Russell of Georgia was one of these, "perhaps the most powerful Senator of his time," recalls Dr. Riddick. "He exerted great influence over the Senate as a whole, but his influence was due to his command of Senate procedure and the respect he enjoyed from his Senate colleagues. On any issue, Russell always had at least thirty votes." Hugh Scott agrees: "Of all the Senators I served with—and there were many—I would say that I believe Russell was the ablest and most influential. He ran his committee with a strong hand, but I don't think anyone ever thought of him as autocratic because he was so highly respected."

## Seniority Weakens

By the 1970s, as we have seen, pressure to modify the seniority system and the power it conferred upon committee chairmen was growing, and both Houses began to institute changes. "What happened in recent years to weaken the seniority system," says Charles Ferris, "is that the turnover ratio is so much greater than in the past. In the early 1980s, I think more than a majority of U.S. Senators were in their first term. The seniority system probably works best when there is an institutional memory among members. When you have the turnover rate you have now there is far less of an institutional memory because people were not there when the building blocks were put together. There's an awful lot of reinventing the wheel because you get an overwhelming majority who are looking at things for the first time. Furthermore, the seniority system fed somewhat upon the new members who were incrementally coming in because they attempted to put value on the seniors who were there. They listened to them, watched what they did and when they did it. There's far less of that today because there are far fewer of those who were around before. If the seniority system is in apparent disfavor, or appears to be weaker, I think it's because the majority has no seniority."

Along with the institutional reforms—both houses now have methods by which party colleagues vote for committee chairmen—more subtle changes have been taking place. "Today a chairman is more apt to listen to his committee than in the past," says former Secretary of the Senate William F. Hildenbrand, "because he can be outvoted—and voted out. He must be accommodating because if he's considered cantankerous he can be replaced. A chairman no longer has the power he had years ago; he no longer can refuse to hold hearings on legislation he opposes. When he did this in the past the committee wouldn't pressure him. The chairman unilaterally determined what bills the committee would consider and the provisions contained in legislation reported out. As the 'old bulls' began to die or retire, the 'new breed' was elected. These younger Senators have no stake in seniority."

Yet, as Paul Duke points out, the seniority system still prevails, especially in the Senate. "Theoretically," Duke says, "a chairman can be thrown out, but actually you'll find the members have a lot of respect for the seniority system because they think that 'if we throw this guy out, it could happen to me.' So, there's an unwritten rule of a sort in the Senate to protect the seniority system."

Former Democratic Congressman Paul G. Rogers of Florida agrees that "seniority was very definitely tighter when I was in Congress than it is today." "Seniority has flexibility now," says former Democratic Congressman George Mahon of Texas, "but prior to 1974 there was practically none. In my opinion, there's too much flexibility, and the chairmen today do not have the feeling of security and stability that I had under the old system. There was good reason to modify the system, but I think the modification has gone a bit too far."

Senator Bumpers would abolish the seniority system. "If I had my way about it," he says, "I would scrap the system because you can have the worst Democrat in the world, the one who is probably the least supportive of Democratic Party positions, move right into the chairmanship of the most powerful committee in the Congress. I think periodically there ought to be at least the threat of a censure on our side—or simply drum them out of the party, saying, 'we don't want you anymore.' I think sometimes people's conduct is bad enough to warrant that kind of Draconian action on our side."

"Seniority is a bad idea, and I'm sorry it got so ingrained," says Congressman Udall. "There was a whole generation when the most important determinant of power in Washington was seniority. In Congress we discourage able younger men and create a system in which consecutive years of tenure are everything and ability, diligence, leadership potential, responsibility count for nothing. Old-timers always comfort us with the crack that 'the seniority system is bad, but the longer you're here the better you'll like it!' But I'm not convinced."

Eugene McCarthy, on the other hand, thinks that the Congress has "quite effectively done away with seniority, and has come close to chaos because of that. As Chesterton said about the Puritans, 'They always kill St. George but keep the dragon.' That's what happened with seniority—they still have the dragon."

"The seniority system obviously has been broken," says Paul Duke. "It's not absolute the way it used to be. When I first went to the Hill as a reporter back in 1959 there were loud screams and complaints against the seniority system. Then a great wave of reform swept across the Capitol and it increased the strength of the Caucus to modify the system. That has been done. The question is whether it has been any better, and I doubt if it has really been any better. The truth is that there just isn't a perfect way to choose a committee chairman."

Not all congressional observers agree that there have been changes, at least in the Senate. "Seniority may have been removed from the written rules," says Anthony Zagami, "but I think it's very much a matter of tradition. The glamour of seniority is still there and the institution itself [the Senate] has a great deal of respect for seniority." James Guirard, former administrative assistant to Senators Russell Long and Allen Ellender of Louisiana, agrees that "the Senate does not operate any differently today than it did when seniority was automatic and absolute. I disagree with those who say the Senate has changed, that the seniority system is no longer as great a force as it was in the past. Today there are different committee chairman. The people have changed, but the institution has not."

Former Republican Senator Marlow Cook of Kentucky recalls that when he first came to the Senate and had no seniority, he thought "maybe something ought to be done and I even proposed limiting terms for members of Congress. I'll never forget Senate

Majority Leader Mike Mansfield kind of taking that pipe out of his mouth, grinning a little bit, and saying, 'Now you are meddling.' Obviously, nothing ever came of it."

> The only thing I didn't like about seniority was that I didn't have enough of it.
>
> —Former Representative Joe D. Waggonner
> (D., Louisiana)

## Notes

1. See Mann and Ornstein, *The New Congress*, p. 33.
2. Legislation must be cleared by the House Rules Committee before it can be taken up by the House of Representatives.

# 4

# The Tide of Change:
# Seniority in Flux

The seniority system no longer makes any difference to the voters.
The electorate looked at seniority and decided it was irrelevant.
Having an effective Senator was significant.
—Nicholas Miller, former Senate aide

By the mid-1970s the seniority system was no longer the central fact of life in the functioning of Congress and changes were occurring throughout—in the rules, in the legislative process, and in the members themselves.[1] As committee chairmen could no longer predicate their power on seniority they became more responsive to other members, and the committees began to function in a more open—though some say less effective—manner. Floor procedure changed too, and in the Senate many bills now were rewritten on the floor, thus circumventing the long-established committee system. Members were more independent, even assertive, and the "democratization" of Congress was underway.

"Seniority has changed a lot, I think, although it's still here," says Senator Chiles. "When I came to the Senate in 1970 I thought there were basically three classes of Senators: the 'big bulls,' the Senators, and the neophytes who were the juniors. I fell into the bottom class. At that time the 'big bulls' were chairmen of the committees, but in addition to being chairmen they were also an interlocking directorate on each other's committees because they also chaired the major subcommittees on each other's committees. The Senators were those who had a major subcommittee, had been here a long time, and were very able. They were probably as able or more able than the 'bulls' who tended to be, you know, ready for the pasture. But they were still there, propped up by their staffs and all. That was just the way the system worked."

"The seniority system no longer is poured into concrete the way we do it now," continues Senator Chiles. "Now, it's historical precedent, so to speak, but it's not in form. Today we have the right at the beginning of a new Congress to elect chairmen and it can be done in a secret ballot if anybody asks for it. One time we went through the process of sort of approving them in a secret ballot, but we stopped that. In fact, now it is almost automatic again. Seniority is honored today, but it is by virtue of habit."

"The seniority system, even though largely weakened and substantially changed from what it once was," says Frank Silbey, "is spread wider now—but thinner. The result is that a new member doesn't have to wait six to eight years for a subcommittee; he'll get a subcommittee chairmanship almost immediately with a small professional staff and a budget. Today there are a lot of smaller barons, thinner mini-principalities."

"The younger member is more active and more interested in the process today," observes Tom Korologos. "They are subcommittee chairmen with a staff and they get active in events. The Vietnam War and Watergate helped bring this about. We'll never see the Senate and the House as they were before."

### The Early Changes: Committees Come into Being

In its first days Congress was primarily a deliberative body in which each house thrashed out the issues of the day in its respective chamber. At this time, the Congress, in Senator Baker's words, was "a citizen's Congress with a full-time chief executive."[2]

If Congress had continued to sit as a collective body, little would have been accomplished. It is the committee system that allows for the presentation of witnesses, debates, legislative drafting sessions, and the printing of reports—all prior to action on the floor where very few pieces of legislation are actually drafted—one very notable exception being the Civil Rights Act of 1964. It was handled on the floor because it could not survive in committee and an aroused public demanded that the Civil Rights bill become law. The power of Congress, acting *en masse* or *en bloc*, is an enormous reserve force, rarely used. When activated—to declare war, for example—it represents a whole country coalesced into one voice.

Basically, all matters are hammered out in committee before the floor vote and the seniority system gives order to the committees and subcommittees, assuring that action is taken, "bunkum"[3] avoided, and some form of continuity is achieved in the legislative process. As members gain experience before assuming chairmanships, they are taken increasingly seriously by their districts, the media, and their colleagues. Their development is important because a chairman—particularly a long-reigning one—is the closest thing to an institutional memory that our government possesses. As the "supergrades" of government employees are lured away by the private sector and as Cabinet officials return to the corporate worlds, the committee chairmen and other senior members of Congress are the ones who remember what went before.

## Chairmen Become Less Autocratic

By the mid-1970s the chairmen—lacking the security that seniority had offered in the past—became increasingly conciliatory toward the views of other committee members. "Chairmen in both houses are more responsive now," says Gaylord Nelson, "because they don't have the power they used to have. When I first came to the Senate in 1963, committee members tended to support their chairmen. That isn't quite so true today. Although the Senate hasn't thrown out any chairmen—as happened in the House—the threat is there because chairmen have to be approved by the caucuses."

"You'll no longer see a man come to Congress and stay for forty years, become a committee chairman, and run his committee like a private province, answerable to no one," says Frank Silbey. "Those days are gone forever."

"Both the House and the Senate have changed their styles dramatically," says Herb Jasper, former Senate committee staffer. "Just making it possible to challenge a chairman forces the chairman to adopt a different style. And the second thing that has happened to erode the influence of seniority is the great dispersal of authority through the subcommittees."

Mace Broide, on the staff of the House Budget Committee and former administrative assistant to Democratic Senator Vance Hartke of Indiana, agrees that the behavior of today's chairman is tempered by the knowledge that he can be unseated. "A chairman must be less autocratic and more accommodating than in the past. This is the difference from fifteen years ago."

A measure of accountability has come into the committee system, according to Fred Wertheimer. "Chairmen now take into account what their colleagues are thinking to a considerable degree."

"Chairmen no longer have anywhere near the authority they had in the past," says Senator Chiles. "Then they had total control over whether or not to schedule a bill or a hearing. They also had total control over their subcommittees, and on some committees, the chairman controlled all the staff."

## Congress Undergoes Change

The geographic base of the congressional power structure also has changed. In the past nearly all committees were chaired by Southerners; today chairmen are elected from diverse parts of the country. "Until a few years ago," says Frank Silbey, "almost the entire committee structure of the Senate was dominated by old Southern committee chairmen. They're almost all gone. Today the old monolithic rural Democratic Party has been destroyed, a two-party system in the Southern states has grown, and there is an increasing black vote."

"The entire membership of both houses has changed as well," Silbey continues. "Members of Congress are younger than their predecessors and are serving fewer terms. Today members of Congress don't hold seats as long as they did in the 'old days,' a generation ago; the turnover is much greater. Also the average age, at least in the Senate, is much lower than it was in the past."

William Hildenbrand feels that "the deciding factor in the shift of power was the changing composition of the Senate: today there are more junior Senators and fewer senior ones and the length of service is shorter. All the changes that have taken place in the Congress have occurred because of the change in the composition of the membership."

"I've seen a number of changes in the Senate," says Senator Byrd, "and one of the most striking is that the overall complexion has changed so dramatically. When I first arrived in the Senate in 1959 all the former Confederate states were represented by Democrats. Today we have quite a number of Southern and border states that no longer are represented by two Democrats each. Secondly, when I came here the Southern Democrats were pretty much welded together on one issue which allowed them to exercise a great deal of clout, perhaps more so than those states are able to exercise today. That situation, plus the fact that so many of the delegations are split, makes it difficult for the Democratic Senators from those states to gain the years of experience—and seniority—to be able to wield as much influence as a region as was the case in those early days. Back then, traditionally, there was more support of the 'establishment' than there is today."

Another change is that some very senior members, veritable fixtures in the Congress, have been rejected by their constituencies. New York Democratic Congressman Emanuel Cellers, reelected for half a century, was a venerable, hardworking, and very senior Congressman. He was well organized and kept his finger on the pulse of his district. Yet Elizabeth Holtzman unseated him. He campaigned on his leadership and seniority but his base had slipped: Many of his supporters had died, retired, or moved from his district; others didn't have the motivation to get out and work the precincts or perhaps they couldn't believe that it was necessary. Fifty years of seniority, in this case, didn't count enough.

There are other changes. Members of Congress today are better educated than was the case in the past and thus, many say, are better qualified to hold national office. "The overall competence of members has risen substantially in the last twenty years or so," says ABC News correspondent Bob Clark, who credits this change, in large part, to television. "Because of television, a bright young fellow—perhaps a crusading district attorney, state attorney general, a lawyer, or whatever in his home state—can be elected outside 'the game under the old rules.' Today through television he can find a way to get in the public eye. Happily there is a fairly close correlation between the way voters perceive a candidate on television and his overall worth, his intellect, and his ability to articulate his views."

The "game under the old rules" to which Clark refers meant that a candidate had to work through a political party to run for national office. "No longer does a candidate work his way up through the local, county, and state levels," explains Mace Broide. "Today an inexperienced candidate can be elected."

"Today new members are better educated, younger, and more aggressive than those of two decades ago," says Patrick O'Donnell, former White House congressional liaison. Lobbyist and former House and Senate staffer Morris Amitay agrees that "the caliber of members of Congress is much better than it was ten or fifteen years ago. Today there are certain minimum standards of competency. Things are getting better."

"The whole climate has changed and there are an awful lot of bright, ambitious young members who are highly respected by their seniors," says CBS newsman George Herman. "A junior member doesn't feel he has to climb for eight or ten years or more before he can say or do anything. That's the way it used to be to a large extent, but it isn't that way anymore. People come right in and start making names for themselves."

"Senators today are probably of a more independent bent than those of the past,"says Senator Byrd. "Moreover, in the past the Senators were more inclined to stand together on issues than is the situation today."

"Today the member of Congress is a lot more intelligent," says Mike Michaelson, for many years superintendent of the House Radio-Television Gallery.[4] "They're a lot brighter and a lot more aware than they were a few years ago. They must be so they can handle national issues, not just local issues. In Congress, unlike in the state legislatures, you're dealing with national issues that affect all citizens, not just citizens of your district or state."

## Other Changes and "Reforms"

Staff hiring became a major power base in the 1970s, and Congress enacted four important reform measures that gave members new authority to hire staff for committee administrative and legislative work. These new staffers worked for the committees but were directly responsible to the members who hired them.[5] Changes in the legislative process were taking place outside the committee as well. In the Senate until a few years ago, the committee version of a bill—its content and language approved by the chairman—used to pass intact. Amendments now are being offered from the floor, "a serious mistake," according to Senator Proxmire. "Legislating from the floor is a great weakness," he says, "because it is so important that we have a record and that we act on the basis of the fullest possible knowledge. When you legislate on the floor, somebody will come up with an amendment you haven't heard of, your staff doesn't know anything about, no hearings have been printed, and no experts have testified. You don't know what the people who really have to live with this legislation think about it and you don't know what the pros and cons are."

Gaylord Nelson agrees that "this is destructive to the committee system which is supposed to have the responsibility for conducting hearings and making a considered judgment on each amendment. Hearings and discussions cannot be conducted on the floor and aren't. Therefore, you adopt some amendments that are very destructive and very costly—[they are] big mistakes and a waste of a lot of time."

Gaylord Nelson gives an example of a Social Security amendment offered on the Senate floor by Frank Church that "just escalated the hell out of the cost of Social Security because nobody recognized one technicality. We knocked that provision out in the 1977 Act that I handled but, in the meantime, we had [given] more benefits to people who had retired in 1976 than to those who had worked the same number of years at the same salary at the same plant but retired a year later . . . which was never intended. Legislating from the floor is a bad idea."

Another change, this one instigated by the reform movements of the 1970s, was the "sunshine law," which opened committee hearings and markups[6] to the public. "It was a time of real democratization," says Nicholas Miller, former counsel to the Senate Commerce Committee. "It may even have been chaotic."

Senator Proxmire supports sunshine laws, even though "they may have slowed down the process a little. Still, I think it's certainly a move in the right direction. This is a big change from when I first came to Congress when all the markups were in executive [closed] sessions, and the press was excluded. Now the markups are all open to the public. This is a democracy, and people have a right to know what goes on in these committees. It's true that the principal people who show up are the lobbyists, and very often the press doesn't show up at all; and if the press doesn't cover a hearing, the public doesn't know about it. But, as time goes on, I think that perhaps the press will show more interest in these open markup sessions and that'll be good."

On the other hand, open hearings and markups create "problems for a lot of people," observes Tom Korologos, "because members have to grandstand a little bit. Also, it has made the damned markups longer than Creation because members have to make the [public] big, fierce fight." Tom Korologos recalls that "one time in Senate Finance there was a markup on a bill with a provision that would benefit Utah but cost zillions of dollars. Senator Wallace Bennett of Utah knew it would be inappropriate to support it because of the great expense and the precedent it would set. So he said, 'Let the record show that I fought fiercely for this amendment' as it went down to defeat. He wasn't about to hurt the country. You need to be able to do some of that internally, but you can't when you have open hearings and open markups. You have to show the folks back home what you're doing."

William Hathaway says he "isn't sure that the open committee markups have proved to be that beneficial. They just drive the members into early morning caucuses to determine what they're going to do before they go out under the floodlights before the public. It just forces another meeting. If they could meet in their markup sessions without the public pressure that comes from open markups they probably could get things through a lot faster and they wouldn't be posing as much."

A further change significantly affecting each member of Congress is the greatly increased workload handled by each office.[7] According to the Postmaster of the House of Representatives, there has been a 2000 percent increase in mail in a little over a decade. In 1970, the Senate and the House combined received 14.6 million pieces of mail; but in 1982, the number had risen to 300 million. The Congressional Management Foundation reports that Hill staffs spend 55 percent of their work time answering correspondence.[8]

"The first year I came here," recalls Gaylord Nelson, "I got about 18,000 letters. My last year in office I got hundreds of thousands— a massive amount of work. Moreover, members are overloaded with nonlegislative matters, and the most popular members spend all their time answering mail, meeting with constituents, going to lunch with them, and doing damned near nothing on the legislative side—and the main purpose of the office is to legislate! You need a better balance between talking to constituents and working on legislation."

The increasing clout of special interest groups is another relatively new and major factor influencing the power balance in Congress. "During the past two decades there has been a great fragmentation in the country and factional groups are seeking to be heard—many of them quite successfully," says Dr. Floyd Riddick. "They've sought change in the government and much of their pressure has been effective."

"The influence of special interest groups and their funding arm, the PACs, has brought about the biggest change in both Houses," says lobbyist Tracy Mullin. "The PAC system has changed lobbying, certainly, and it has changed the way a lot of members vote and respond to requests from lobbyists and their constituents. The development of the interest group lobby has meant that unless you have a lot of money behind you, your're not going to get anywhere."

"I think that the tremendous power of the PAC has probably had a lot to do with making Congress ineffective," says Senator Chiles. "Each controls a little box of power. They come against each other, there's no doubt about it. There are enough PACs so that it sort of neutralizes everything. It's better just to play it safe, and not get out front on anything because you might lose your money. I think PACs have had a profound influence on what's going on now. I'm very much against that."

Perhaps there have been too many changes, suggests Harley Dirks, former administrative assistant to Democratic Senator Warren Magnuson of Washington. "The reforms have made it so they can't produce meaningful legislation anymore, and all these changes have caused Congress to go in a bad direction. The Hill has become a huge bureaucracy with huge staffs, and today Congress is cumbersome, overburdened with employees, issues, and committees. Congress no longer makes political decisions, rather, it makes bureaucratic decisions because it has become a bureaucracy. Congress just isn't fun anymore."

But Senator Bumpers, on the other hand, disagrees: "Things haven't changed around here very dramatically at all. I came to the Senate in 1973 and I've seen it before and after. I have come to believe that a lot of things I hear expressed by some of the older members—that things have changed so dramatically—are pure poppycock. I'm convinced that things are as good, or even better, than they used to be. Will Rogers used to say 'Things ain't like they used to be an' they never were,' and that's the way I feel about the Senate."

Paul Duke, who has reported on Congress for the *Wall Street Journal*, NBC News, and public television, says that "one of the things that really strikes me is that when I first went to the Hill as a reporter there was all this disgruntlement about the way Congress operated and there were calls for rules changes to make it more democratic—and they changed it. They finally won that fight. Now there are complaints that one of the effects of this is that too many people have too much power. So now power is diffused. The question is: What is the best way? I am not so sure but that it didn't work better in the old days when Judge Howard Smith, Chairman of Rules, Republican leader Charlie Halleck, and Speaker Rayburn would go into a room and strike a deal. Today there is just chaos."

> There is a price to pay for all these changes: Congress has become an unruly mob.
>
> —Assistant to a prominent member of Congress
> who wishes to remain anonymous

## Notes

1. See Norman Ornstein et al., "The Senate Through the 1980s: Cycles of Change," *Congress Reconsidered*, pp. 13–33.

2. *The New York Times Magazine*, April 11, 1984.

3. The word "bunkum" comes from the great debates in the Compromise of 1820. The gentleman from Bunkum County, North Carolina, talked endlessly and uninformedly, and thus the word was coined.

4. Michaelson is currently vice-president of C-SPAN, the television network that broadcasts House debates over cable television.

5. The Legislative Reorganization Act of 1970 increased from four to six the number of professional aides who could be employed by most standing committees in each house. The minority party was authorized to hire one third. The House Committee Amendments of 1974 tripled the size of most House standing committee staffs, with the minority party allowed to ap-

point one third. Senate Resolution 60 authorized each Senator to hire up to three committee assistants. The Senate Committee Amendments of 1977 required the size of each committee staff to be in proportion to the number of majority and minority members on each standing committee, allocating at least one third of the funds to the minority.

6. Legislative drafting sessions.

7. See Norman Ornstein et al., *Vital Statistics on Congress* (Washington, D.C.: American Enterprise Institute, 1984), pp. 138–152.

8. See Lewis Anthony Dexter, "What Do Congressmen Hear?" in *Congressional Behavior*, p. 28.

# 5

# Committee Assignments: A Start Up the Ladder

I think a committee assignment really means more than any single thing to a member of Congress and has more to do with his future than anything else.

—Former Congressman Frank Ikard

When Congress organized in 1789 neither house established permanent committees. Instead, each chamber handled legislation on the floor, appointing a temporary committee for every bill and dissolving it when the legislation was voted upon. However, because this method proved cumbersome—for example, during the Third Congress, 1793–1795, approximately 350 such committees were created—permanent standing committees were gradually established, each having jurisdiction over a specialized area.[1]

The Congress has three principal kinds of committees:

- Standing Committees, which are permanent, have the power to write legislation and report bills to the floor.
- Select or Special Committees, usually temporary, are created to study special problems. They have investigative powers and rarely report bills.
- Joint Committees, composed of members from both houses, have an investigative function and are created to examine public problems or review programs. Joint committees rarely report bills.

In addition, conference committees, composed of members from both houses and established on an *ad hoc* basis, resolve differences between legislation reported from both houses.[2]

The first standing committee, the House Committee on Elections, was established in 1789, and by 1810 nine more had been added. The Senate, creating only four committees in its first twenty-five years, handled most of its work through select committees. However, by the first half of the 19th century, the standing committee system was entrenched firmly in both houses, and during the second half of the 19th and into the 20th centuries, the number of committees rose rapidly, to be diminished periodically by reorganizations and consolidations. In the 98th Congress (1983–1985) the structure was as follows:

*House Standing Committees*: Argriculture; Appropriations; Armed Services; Banking, Finance, and Urban Affairs; Budget; District of Columbia; Education and Labor; Energy and Commerce; Foreign Affairs; Government Operations; House Administration; Interior and Insular Affairs; Judiciary; Merchant Marine and Fisheries; Post Office and Civil Service; Public Works and Transportation; Rules; Science and Technology; Small Business; Standards of Official Conduct; Veteran's Affairs; Ways and Means.

*House Select Committees*: Aging, Children, Youth, and Families; Hunger; Intelligence (permanent); Narcotics, Abuse and Control.

*Senate Standing Committees*: Agriculture, Nutrition, and Forestry; Appropriations; Armed Services; Banking, Housing, and Urban Affairs; Budget; Commerce, Science, and Transportation; Energy and Natural Resources; Environment and Public Works; Finance; Foreign Relations; Governmental Affairs; Judiciary; Labor and Human Resources; Rules and Administration; Small Business; Veterans Affairs.

*Senate Select Committees*: Ethics; Indian Affairs; Intelligence.

*Senate Special Committee*: Aging.

*Joint Committees of Congress*: Economic; Library; Printing; Taxation.

## Committee Assignment Procedures

Both the House and the Senate appoint members of committees through chamber approval of a list of names submitted by party leaders. This procedure, adopted by the Senate in 1846 and the House in 1911, takes place at the beginning of each new Congress, when new members are assigned to committees and vacancies caused by death, retirement, or transfer to another committee are filled.

In the Senate, the leaders of both parties offer floor resolutions on committee assignments which usually are adopted automatically by the full chamber. The rosters are prepared by the Senate Democratic Steering Committee, chaired by the party leader who names the other Steering Committee members, and the Republican Committee on Committees, appointed by the chairman of the Republican Conference. (The Republican Caucus does not vote on committee nominations.)

In the House, the Democratic Steering and Policy Committee prepares a list, subject to Caucus approval.[3] House Republican nominations are chosen by their Committee on Committees, composed of one representative from each state having at least one Republican in its House delegation, and the House Republican Policy Committee must approve the choices. Then, as in the Senate, the full chamber votes on the lists. (The House has an exception: the Rules Committee. In 1975, the Speaker was given the power to nominate all Democratic members of Rules, subject to ratification by the Caucus).[4]

The major factors considered in making committee appointments include a member's personal choice, a committee's geographical balance, seniority, and party loyalty. According to William Hildenbrand, "the leadership can impose its will on members by rewarding or denying committee positions, and the leaders have the authority to give 'plums,' or preferred assignments," to loyal party members.

## Obtaining the Committee Assignment

How does a member ensure a desirable committee assignment? "You talk to the leadership; you talk to the Committee on Committees," explains William Hathaway, "and you have to be fairly aggressive about it."

"You try to enlist the help of your delegation," says Frank Ikard. "I know when I used to be involved in that [as a member of Ways and Means, the Democratic Committee on Committees] it was entirely different because we always met with the leadership. We would go over the list of the new members and those members who wanted to change committees. The Speaker and the Majority Leader had a great deal of influence and it would just be a matter of working it out among the members of the Committee on Committees. There was a lot of lobbying going on with lots of groups—labor, agriculture, this group, that group—who always had people they wanted on particular committees. So it was a tough thing to do."

House Republicans, points out Barber Conable, "worked it out [so] that there would be a yes or no vote by secret ballot of the entire conference on the nominations of the Committee on Committees for chairmanships. It was generally assumed that the senior member would be nominated and that's the way it has worked. We have not had the ceremonial executions that the Democrats did when they adopted something very similar to our rule in response to public pressure four years after we did. They eventually were dragged kicking and screaming into doing pretty much the same thing we are doing, having a secret ballot vote by the Caucus. In other words, we have a pretty good system in the Republican Party. Now that the Ways and Means Committee is no longer the Democrat's Committee on Committees—the Speaker has a steering committee—lots of the Democrats want to challenge the issue. Of course, committee leadership means more to them than it does to us because they are the majority."

"The most important ingredient by far for a Senator in getting a committee assignment is what he wants," says Senator Proxmire. "Senators will usually get what they want if they are persistent enough and keep after it. When they first come in they may not get it, unless, of course, they come in at a time when it is important to their party to hold a majority; then they'll often see that a Senator gets an assignment that will be helpful to him in getting reelected. That's one of the strongest arguments a Senator can make. The Steering Committee itself decides and Senators lobby the Steering Committee."

Gale McGee tells of the unusual reason he was assigned to the Senate Appropriations Committee, becoming the first member to serve on that committee who had no prior government experience. "That wasn't any tribute to me, I discovered," McGee says. "Three experienced Senators were applying for one vacancy: Stu Symington, Hubert Humphrey, and Jack Kennedy. At that time the leader had great power in assigning committees, and I like to think that [then Senate Majority Leader] Lyndon Johnson saw that I would be a great influence and he ought to start building me up in there.

But Lyndon had rationalized that there are three good guys and
we cannot give the assignment to one without making an enemy
of the other two. Therefore, we'll leave them all out and pick
McGee. Well, that was only part of the story. What neophyte
McGee didn't know then was that Lyndon had already made his
decision to run gung-ho for President, and he wasn't going to build
up one of his possible competitors. That's how Gale McGee got in
there—in spite of any seniority considerations."

## The Important Committees

Control of revenues and expenditures, according to Senator
McClure, is the reason many members choose the Appropriations,
Senate Finance, or House Ways and Means Committees. "Traditionally, the appropriations process is important [as a committee
assignment]. Because it controls money, the process affects things
that are important to a member or to his district in a very parochial
sense. A member of Appropriations can have an impact on a broad
range of politics in a way that members of other committees can't.
Also, in recent years, the Senate Finance Committee has become
perhaps even more important than the House Appropriations
Committee because Finance now affects more programs and more
expenditures than Appropriations."

In addition, Senator McClure says that the visibility a committee can afford a member is a prime concern and the Senate Foreign Relations Committee may be chosen for that reason. "Senate
Foreign Relations has been a political plus for years," he says, "because it creates national personalities." Taft, however, tells another
side of serving on Foreign Relations: "When I served on Senate
Foreign Relations with [New York Republican Senator] Jack Javits
for six years," Taft relates, "he hogged the staff and hogged the
limelight. It was his nature and there wasn't anything bitter as we
were close personal friends. But it was hard to make much hay one
way or the other on an issue or as an individual or make a headline
so far as the committee was concerned because Jack had complete
control over everything."

"The committee's importance depends on what you want to do
for your state," says Senator Chiles. "Some Senators feel they never
have to be concerned about their states and just involve them-

selves with national issues; others spend all their time trying to do something for their state. However, most of us are somewhere in between and feel an obligation to try to see that we get our share of the 'pork.' Of course, we don't call it pork when we're getting it for our state. But committees become very important that way. I'm on the Transportation Subcommittee of Appropriations, so I'm in a place to see that Florida is considered with regard to public roads, highways, people movers, studies on bullet trains, and things like that. I'm also very concerned about the drug situation. On Appropriations I do what I can to help the Coast Guard and Customs in that area. So, depending on what your interest is—and you tend to try to get on committees or subcommittees where your major interest is—you can influence policy."

"A committee assignment is very important to a member of the Senate or the House of Representatives," says Senator Robert Byrd. "The member hopes to be appointed to a committee which can be most helpful in his congressional district or his state, whichever the case may be. In my case, it was helpful to me to be on the Committee on Appropriations. Therefore, I asked Lyndon Johnson, who was Senate Majority Leader when I came here in January 1959, for an assignment on the Appropriations Committee, a highly cherished committee assignment. I've been able to do a lot on the Appropriations Committee in these twenty-six years [in the Senate] for West Virginia. And the same thing would be true of other members."

Robert Taft calls the Armed Services Committee a "plus," but says he "could be cynical and call it a 'pork barrel' committee because you can take care of your state and get defense contracts, and at the same time deal with international issues which are important. The House Armed Services Committee was considered so important that Carl Vinson of Georgia, its chairman for fourteen years [1949–1953; 1955–1965], replied when asked why he was interested in becoming Secretary of Defense, 'Why should I? It's easier to run the Defense Department from here!' "

How quickly a member can become a chairman is "of considerable importance," says Taft, "and the committees you get on determine that. It may not be what committee you become chairman of—so long as it is a fairly important committee—but how long it takes you to become chairman." Senator Bumpers agrees that "because of the seniority system, we're always reluctant to change committees. That's unfortunate because if I had to do it all over again, I wouldn't have taken the committee assignments I did. If, on the other hand, you're looking at the politics of a committee assignment," he says, "you have to be cognizant of the fact that some people just get lucky. For example, during a particular term of Congress, the Judiciary Committee might be the most important committee, especially if there are two or three hotly contested Supreme Court appointments or constitutional amendments. Or if you were to have an oil embargo out of the Middle East, then the Energy Committee would loom very large. So, the importance of a committee assignment could be determined by pure luck."

> A committee assignment's importance depends on what you mean by importance. If you mean important in the sense of getting re-elected, it can be very important.
>
> —Senator William Proxmire

## Notes

1. See Norman Ornstein, et al., *Vital Statistics on Congress*, pp. 105–115.

2. Because a bill must be passed by both Houses in identical form, the chairmen of the House and Senate standing committees handling a given piece of legislation appoint a conference committee—usually, but not always, composed of the most senior members of each committee—to work out differences.

3. Until 1975 Democratic committee assignments were made by the Democratic Committee on Committees, composed of the Democratic members of the Ways and Means Committee.

4. See Nicholas A. Masters, "Committee Assignments," in *Congressional Behavior*, p. 153.

# 6

# Leadership, Loyalty, and Seniority

We used to have giants, but we live in an age today without strong leadership.

—Morris Amitay, Washington lobbyist
and former congressional staffer

As the absolute hold of the seniority system began to loosen, other changes were taking place in the Congress, most notably a decline in the leadership's ability to control the legislative process.[1] Party discipline, which had been exercised so successfully in the past, was giving way to a new independence among members of both houses, and by the 1980s the term "party position" was fast becoming an anachronism.

"Party loyalty, party discipline, and party positions are almost totally gone," says Senator McClure. "Parties, in order to have strength and authority and discipline have to be able to do for, or to, members things that are important to them. The party doesn't deliver much anymore. Senatorial campaign committees and national committees can do more for members than was possible in the past. The power is used sparingly but it's there."

Senator Bumpers wants party leadership and party discipline strengthened. "I am absolutely appalled at what we tolerate on our side of the aisle," Bumpers says. "Some Democratic Senators vote against a party position when it would have absolutely no effect on them back home. I can understand somebody covering his flank politically in order to accommodate the interests back home; nobody really falls out with that. What I do object to are a few peo-

ple, at least on our side of the aisle, who consistently vote against
the party position—and that's usually enough to keep us from pre-
vailing or at least making a significant show on party positions. I
think periodically there ought to be times when you censure members of your own party."

Former Democratic Congressman Richard Bolling of Missouri
says that "no one should ever put a guy on a first-rate committee—
one of the top four—unless he understands you expect him to be
a party member. I don't think he ought to have that privilege. But
once you put him on, if he betrays you, you ought to cut his throat."
However, Bolling stresses that this "doesn't mean the party ex-
pects you to cut your throat in your district. That's where the cut-
line is, as far as I'm concerned."

According to Bolling, "The higher an honor—or privilege or power
or what the hell you call it—the more loyalty is expected. I don't
believe in slaves and I wouldn't be one myself. I have been out-
spoken against the whole party on occasion. But, by and large, the
higher the position, the more loyalty is demanded."

"The partial dissolution of the seniority system has cost the Congress a great deal as an institution," says Dan Thomasson, whose
long career as a Washington journalist culminated in his appointment as the Scripps-Howard Washington bureau chief. "I think
any administration has to realize that congressional leaders aren't
in full control anymore. For instance, today you cannot count on a
Speaker of the House to control his troops as you once could."

"The House works much better when there is both a strong
Speaker and a strong committee system," said Frank Ikard. "I can't
think of a legislative body in the world that can operate without
procedure controlled by some kind of organizational mechanism
headed by a Speaker or whatever they call it. The House is so
diffused now, with no central authority anymore, that it has become ineffective."

Former Transportation Secretary Alan Boyd "would like to see
party discipline return because it's quite important for party health,
and I think that party health is a very important thing in this country if, over the long run, we're going to avoid splinter parties."

"The parties have been dead for years," says Tom Korologos.
"Finished. There no longer are party positions and party votes and
the reason party positions no longer work is because of the inde-

pendence of the Representatives and Senators." William Hathaway
thinks that "members of Congress probably have a better chance
of winning elections if they can parade themselves as being inde-
pendents, whereas in years past people generally aligned themselves with a political party."

William Hildenbrand agrees that "party loyalty is no longer a
factor. In the past, legislators first served their parties as state
chairmen, party chairmen, precinct captains, and so forth. They
had been in politics in their states for a long time and were 'party-
structured.' They would come up through the ranks until the party
determined it was their turn to run for the House or the Senate.
Party discipline was easy to maintain because they were party ori-
ented. Today many members of Congress never entered politics
until they ran for the House or the Senate. Party loyalty doesn't
exist and neither does party discipline."

"There's no party discipline anymore," agrees former Senator
Marlow Cook. "It doesn't really mean anything to be aligned with
one party or the other today because the real issue isn't whether
you're a party individual or not but whether you can get reelected."

"There has been a decline in party positions and party strength
because each individual member has a greater say now than he
had before," says Paul Rogers. "Also, a member's obligation to his
party is somewhat different now, I think. There's more independence and, for the most part, less dependence on party organizations. Politicians can assert more independence and they do."

"The leadership in the Congress has been pretty much emascu-
lated," said Frank Church. "I don't know whether it is possible for
the leadership to regain its authority, to reestablish itself, now that
the members have sort of 'cut loose.' "

The new visibility and increased activity of freshmen Senators is
a major change, Church said. "It was very rare indeed in the past
that freshmen Senators ventured onto the floor during their first
year in office to propound seriously on major public issues. Today
the freshman Senators are talking all the time about everything,
consuming enormous amounts of time but really not adding very
much to the wisdom of the institution."

Church cited the growing number of roll call votes as an example of diminished party discipline. "When I first entered the Sen-

ate there were perhaps maybe a fourth as many roll call votes as
there are today. The reason for this was that the leadership decided when there was to be a roll call and individual members
customarily did not demand roll calls for every amendment. It just
wasn't done. The Senate would not stand up if an individual member asked for a roll call and the leadership hadn't indicated that it
was all right. Now anybody can get a roll call any time he wishes.
I think the last year I was in the Senate I must have voted twenty-
four times on abortion alone—for political purposes to build up
statistical ammunition to be used against an opponent in the next
election."

"How many votes on abortion do you need in one session?" asks
Gaylord Nelson. "On every bill that comes along—bang!—another
amendment on abortion or school prayer or something else. All
that is requiring too much time in the Congress."

Seniority's decline may not be the only reason for the inability
of the leadership to exercise discipline, according to Melvin Laird.
Laird says that the proliferation of staff added to the weakening of
the parties in Congress. "Too many people are working in the
Congress who are thinking up ideas to get their members on the
evening news or into the magazines and newspapers, and too many
staffers have ideas for legislation. These staff people are looking
out just for their members, not for the Congress. There's no party
loyalty, discipline, or cohesion, and the institution has suffered."
The Senate Foreign Relations Committee and its staff alone currently outnumber the entire membership and staff of both houses
of the First Congress.

William Hathaway feels that it isn't possible to exercise party
discipline in either house today. "I think you just have to live with
the situation," he says, "and hope that someday the members
themselves will wake up to the fact that this is getting nowhere."

## Strong Leaders: Rayburn and Johnson

The absence of strong leaders in Congress is cited frequently as
a major contributing factor to the decline of party power. Dynamic
men like Speaker Rayburn and Senate Majority Leader Lyndon
Johnson, it is said, were able to maintain strict party discipline
through sheer force of personality.[2] Their successors, in contrast,

were much weaker men and thus unable to contain the growing assertiveness among members of Congress. "Strong leadership depends on personality a great deal," says Dan Thomasson, "and the days of strong, overwhelming speakers and majority leaders are gone. We're never going back to the days when they called the turn of everything, that's just not going to happen."

The Speaker of the House is "first in the land," wrote Congressman Richard Bolling in *House Out of Order* (1965). "He receives elaborate homage and respect; but he is dependent on the powerful lords, usually committee chairmen." Sam Rayburn, the longest serving Speaker in history, from 1940–1953 and from 1955 to his death in 1961, came to office at a time when long careers were the rule, and his success was due partially to the seniority system as well as his own ability to establish a delicate balance of power between committee chairmen and the party leadership, forming coalitions and working out compromises. "When Sam Rayburn was Speaker, there was tremendous party discipline and everybody wanted to go with him," recalls Wilbur Mills. "Rayburn's power was the strength of his personality," says Hugh Scott. "He was a very strong man and he knew how to be effective."

Former Congressman Bolling talks about Rayburn's attitude toward seniority: "With Rayburn you weren't going to get much said overtly in relation to seniority, but he was rather interesting in the way he moved about the edges. For example, Rayburn wanted to get control of the Un-American Activities Committee—he didn't want to abolish it, but to get it into reasonably responsible and friendly hands. So he worked out devices that would knock out the real extremists. Instead of modifying seniority [to keep the extremists off the committee], Rayburn declared that to be a member of the Un-American Activities Committee you had to be a former judge. That effectively prevented the extremists from sitting on the committee while avoiding violating the seniority system."

"Rayburn was able to use power properly," says Melvin Laird, telling of the time Rayburn gave him a "hideaway" office near the House dining room. "He could have given that office to a Democrat but he called me into his office one day and said, 'Mel, I just like the way you operate out on the floor and I'd like you to have your own little dining room.' Today the Speaker has lost many of the things that are needed to maintain his authority."

"The constant presence of Sam Rayburn," recalls Gale McGee, "was almost as important—maybe more important—than that of Lyndon Johnson because Rayburn was looked up to by everybody including Lyndon as the master craftsman in the American legislative system. At one stage—either 1958 or 1960—Johnson had fifty-one Senators who had previously served in the House. Rayburn always needled Lyndon about that: 'Whom do you think has the most votes in the Senate?' Rayburn would ask him."

Frank Ikard describes Rayburn's style: "He would sit down in the evening in that office of his in the Capitol, 'the Board of Education,' with committee chairmen and usually the Senate Majority Leader. They would make up the legislative agenda very informally—it wasn't etched in stone or anything—and over a little bourbon and branch water they would sit down and talk and resolve any problems. Rayburn had a theory that I heard him express many times. He said there was one caucus [during] each Congress and that was when they elected him Speaker. From there on in, he would make the decisions. Rayburn was an impressive person and I think his personality was greater than his real authority—but no one ever wanted to test that to see if it were true."

"How much is due to the personality and how much due to the power of the office?" asks Wayne Thevenot, former legislative assistant to Democratic Senator Russell Long of Louisiana. During the years that Lyndon B. Johnson was Majority Leader, Thevenot recalls, "it was hard to determine when the office exerted its inherent powers or when Johnson was maneuvering in 'the Johnson style.'"

Senator Proxmire recalls that when he first came to the Senate, it was "really run" by the Majority Leader. "He made every kind of decision," Proxmire says, "and that hasn't been true since Johnson left. The strength of personality of the leader has a lot to do with it, and if you have a Majority Leader who's anxious for power and anxious to exert power the way Johnson was then that's the way it goes; party discipline was strong when Johnson was leader because he was a strong leader." Proxmire points out, however, that it wasn't partisan power that Johnson exercised, "it was a 'Johnsonian' power."[3]

Until Johnson became the leader of the Democrats in 1953, Senate committee chairmen were unchallenged, exercising total control over legislation both in committee and on the floor. Chairmen also determined the scheduling of bills, merely informing the leadership when to call for a vote. The main function of the Senate Majority Leader was to assure that members of his party voted "correctly," except perhaps on noncontroversial legislation emerging from minor committees.

Lyndon Johnson changed that. While his position as Majority Leader[4] gave him no more authority than that of his predecessors, he implemented it in a much different manner. "Johnson's strength lay not in any rules," says Gaylord Nelson, "he just spent full time on hard work, either persuading or intimidating or pushing—using every device at hand to get people to go along with him."

Johnson dispensed favors to other Senators, a practice designed to obligate them to him, as well as to dilute the power of the most senior members. "Johnson really loved to exercise power, and he exercised it," notes George Herman. "Johnson always said, 'Let us reason together,' but when you reasoned together with Johnson he would pull out of his pocket a handful of chits and say, 'Remember I voted with you on this and I supported you on that, and I damned well expect you to vote for me on this.' Johnson had a very result-oriented psychology."

Herman tells about the time a group of liberal Senators, headed by Senator Abraham A. Ribicoff (D., Connecticut), was speaking in support of a bill on the Senate floor. "Johnson was standing outside talking to reporters," Herman recalls, "and he shook his head and said, 'What's the matter with those idiots? Can't they count?' Johnson saw no point in wasting the Senate's time talking for a bill if you had not already counted the votes. And if you didn't have the votes, why bother the Senate with speaking about some bill? Johnson figured it was wasted if you did not have the votes in your pocket before you went on the floor. He was really a very, very tough man."[5]

"The strong leadership of LBJ in the Senate," says Charles Ferris, "was possible because he was a consummate political animal. He lived the institution. He was very, very interested in the personalities of the members. However, his leadership was predicated upon a great deal of 'followship' and abdication of individual responsibilities."

Johnson's changes included the practice of allowing junior members more participation in the legislative process, violating the custom that a Senator was not to deliver a speech on the floor during his first year. However, it was what became known as the Johnson Rule that brought the most striking change to the Senate. Adopted by the Senate Democrats in 1953, the Johnson Rule provided that no member of the party, regardless of his seniority, would receive a second top committee assignment until every Democratic Senator had been given at least one such assignment. This change not only permitted junior members to serve on the important committees, it lessened the near monopoly senior members held on the power derived from prestigious assignments. A few years later, the Republicans adopted a modified version of the Johnson Rule. (In 1959, the Republicans, at that time the minority party, adopted a rule that limited a Senator to one ranking committee slot.)

Although the Johnson Rule was a major factor in the breakdown of the seniority system in the Senate, it was not, according to John McConnell, Johnson's motive in allowing junior Senators to receive top committee assignments. Rather it was a method Johnson used to strengthen his control. "The Johnson Rule was the turning point in the Senate," says Mace Broide. "It was the watershed that broke down the barriers for freshmen Senators."

"The Johnson Rule opened the door," says Fred Wertheimer. "Johnson was representing the Democratic Party and this was a way to give junior members more power. It also was a smart thing to do. It meant that 'the action was going to be spread around' and it put Johnson in the position of being the one to do the spreading."

"I don't think that Lyndon Johnson or Sam Rayburn would have been able to operate with the kind of system we have now," says Haynes Johnson. "No longer are the leaders given absolute power. The fact is that the leadership doesn't have more power today. Just because in theory the leadership can throw out a chairman, it doesn't work that way. I think, across the board, the political climate has changed."

Senator Proxmire does not miss Johnson's strong leadership: "I would not want to bring back a Lyndon Johnson. I thought that was terrible, the worst possible situation. Nobody in Wisconsin voted for a Majority Leader from Texas. Things can function pretty well with undisciplined parties which allow members to make up their own minds on the issues."

"I believe in strong leadership in a legislative body," says Frank Ikard. "You have to have it if you're going to be able to have a legislative program that moves. I don't think that the present leadership is weak; they just don't have the rules that let them be leaders."

"The problem," said Howard Baker, when he was Senate Majority Leader, "is what I call the 'wet noodle problem,' and that is I cannot make the Senate do anything it does not want to do."[6]

Most congressional observers agree with George Herman that "we're going to find that you can't run a Congress with five hundred thirty-five different members going their own ways. There has to be some party leadership, some party cohesiveness. It doesn't seem that fragmenting has been terribly successful. Eventually people who have experienced this lack of leadership are going to say, 'This is no way to run a railroad.' "

> A leader can't be a nice guy. He's got to be a bastard because he must make the trains run on time.
>
> —Tom C. Korologos

## Notes

1. See Roger H. Davidson, "Senate Leaders: Janitors for an Untidy Chamber," in *Congress Reconsidered*, pp. 225–250.

2. See John G. Steward, "Two Strategies of Leadership: Johnson and Mansfield," in *Congressional Behavior*, p. 61.

3. Michael Foley, *The New Senate* (New Haven: Yale University Press, 1980), pp. 23–25.

4. Beginning in 1955.

5. See Robert L. Peabody, *Leadership in Congress* (Boston: Little, Brown and Company, 1976), p. 341.

6. Quoted in the *New York Times*, November 14, 1983, p. 34.

# 7

# Ways and Means: An Example of Longevity and Power

All Bills for raising Revenues shall originate in the House of Representatives.

—Constitution of the United States,
article 1, section 7, clause 1

Few committees were untouched by the reform movement that coursed through the Congress in the 1970s. Even the House Ways and Means Committee, perhaps the most powerful committee in the Congress, could not remain immune to the attacks on the seniority system. It may, in fact, have emerged the most radically changed.

The Ways and Means Committee, established by the House on July 24, 1789, was granted authority to write and alter the tax laws of the nation.[1] Two months later, however, it was dissolved and until 1795 all fiscal and monetary legislation was drafted by the Treasury Department. To regain control of the nation's fiscal policy, the Congress in 1795 reestablished Ways and Means as a permanent committee, and seven years later it formally achieved standing committee status. Its jurisdiction covered both revenue and appropriations legislation until an Appropriations Committee was created in 1865. Its control over revenues remains to this day.[2]

Thus, since the end of the 18th century, Ways and Means has had authority over all legislation concerning taxes, Social Security, tariffs, unemployment compensation, national health insurance, public assistance, and Medicare—the country's "pocketbook" issues. In addition, from 1911 to 1975, it was also the Democratic

Committee on Committees, entrusted with making all of its party's House committee assignments. It was a powerful authority that could be used to reward loyalty or coerce support.

## Wilbur Mills

Democratic Congressman Wilbur Mills of Arkansas, considered one of the most powerful—if not the most powerful—committee chairmen, was elected to Ways and Means in 1942 and served as chairman from 1958 until his resignation, under pressure, in 1975.[3] Mills was highly respected for his thorough knowledge of the nation's tax code but his chairmanship, and thus his power, derived from the seniority system.

He exercised tight control over his committee, abolishing all subcommittees when he took office in 1958, a move that increased the power of the chairman. He also obtained a closed rule from Chairman Judge Smith of the House Rules Committee, thereby ensuring that no amendments from the floor would be allowed on Ways and Means bills. Only amendments from within the committee were permitted, and the floor vote could be solely yea or nay on the intact committee bill. Very few Ways and Means tax bills were rejected during Mills' chairmanship. In addition, Mills' legislation was given "priviliged" status, allowing it to be taken up by the House ahead of other bills.

"I tried to master everything that came through my committee," Mills said eight years after his retirement. "When I first got there, Rayburn told me 'If you're going to have members listen to you, make them think you know what you're talking about which means you've got to know what you're talking about. You must learn the jurisdiction of your committee—not every committee, but your own committee.' "

"Wilbur Mills was recognized for his enormous virtuosity and skill," says Maurice Rosenblatt, "and he was the only man who knew the tax code in and out. Everyone deferred to his knowledge. He had enormous power because, in addition to Ways and Means, he was head of the Committee on Committees, meaning he had power over your House career. He could put you on Merchant Marine and Fisheries, for example, if you wanted to be on Agriculture. You didn't particularly want to be on the wrong side of Wilbur Mills, but he was not a vindictive man, as were some other powerful chairmen who kept book and punished people."

UPI House Bureau Chief Don Phillips remembers Mills as "a consensus chairman." He was smart enough to know that he had to please his committee. He would sit there and listen for three, four, or five days while the other members talked to see which way the wind was blowing. If he didn't agree with them, he could kill whatever the proposal was if he couldn't change it. However, if he agreed or at least was amenable, one day he'd just drop the gavel and say, 'This is what we're going to do.' For that he got the reputation of being a tyrant, the powerful committee chairman who would kick his committee around. That's wrong. He was just smart enough to see what his committee was doing; yet nobody ever challenged Wilbur. He used to keep that committee in his hip pocket."

"He always managed to make it look as if there were a consensus," recalls George Herman. "He was extremely powerful because he studied hard and knew everything so well that he could—with a judicious combination of delay and education, I guess you would call it—get his way most of the time."

"Wilbur Mills had a great knack for reconciling differences," says Paul Duke. "I remember during the time that I covered Ways and Means for the *Wall Street Journal* in the early 1960s that Mills would never take a bill to the floor unless he was certain the bill was going to be approved. He'd try to accommodate all viewpoints. Obviously you can't always, but he could accommodate enough to bring out a consensus product that would get through. Over and beyond that Wilbur himself had a lot of his colleagues' respect as the foremost tax and revenue expert in Congress. For Mills to get up on the floor and speak on behalf of something almost certainly would assure its acceptance."

## A Committee Under Fire

Many of the legislative reforms of the 1970s, especially the Hansen proposals,[4] were directed at the structure and methods of the Ways and Means Committee—the absence of subcommittees, its closed meetings, and its protection from floor amendments. In 1975 the House adopted a provision that required all committees with more than fifteen members to have at least four subcommittees, and Ways and Means established subcommittees on welfare, trade, Social Security, unemployment compensation, health, and special revenue."I was the only chairman who recommended subcommittees to the Hansen Committee," recalled Mills later."I was tired and worn out doing all the work. I tried to get my own committee to let me set up some subcommittees in January 1973 but they turned me down—rather, not turned me down, but said, 'Everything is going fine, Wilbur, why don't you just leave it alone? You're satisfied.' So, I dropped the subject."

Another reform that directly attacked the power of Ways and Means provided that fifty or more members of the Democratic Caucus could request the leadership to order the Rules Committee to draft an open rule; thus, the Congress now could alter any and all Ways and Means Committee legislation. Again the rules were changed in 1975 to require that all Ways and Means revenue bills receive a specific place on the docket and could no longer come before other legislation to the floor—thus revoking "privileged" status.

Subsequently, the Ways and Means Committee was enlarged from twenty-five to thirty-seven members and the 3:2 Democratic margin increased to 2:1, reflecting Democratic gains in the previous election. The twelve new members and the creation of subcommittees effectively dispersed power throughout the committee. In addition the Ways and Means Committee's jurisdiction over revenue-sharing legislation was given to Government Operations and its export control authority went to Foreign Affairs. A final erosion of its power took place with the creation of the Budget Committee which assumed responsibility for coordinating revenue legislation from Ways and Means with expenditures, the province of Appropriations.

As criticism of the seniority system and the power it conferred upon chairmen increased, more reforms were enacted, and the authority of Ways and Means Democrats to make their party's committee appointments was transferred to a much broader-based Steering and Policy Committee.[5] Mills recalls nearly a decade later that he "didn't fight it. I didn't have any interest in fighting it. It was a thankless job. You made people mad at you if they didn't get the committee they wanted. I didn't care one way or the other—

some members of the committee did, but I didn't." Mills said the change "put the Speaker in complete control of assignments, which adds to his strength; but he has to take the blame for all that goes wrong and gets very little credit when it does go right. They're going back in the direction from which they came, it looks to me. It's done by liberals, more or less. I don't know why."

The reforms requiring open committee sessions took effect, and by 1975, 98 percent of Ways and Means hearings and markups, or legislative drafting sessions, were open, compared with 70 percent in 1973. "Today, Ways and Means no longer can expect to have closed rules, to dominate the Rules Committee decisions, or to have an automatic presumption of floor acceptance," said Barber Conable in 1984, when he was ranking Republican on the Ways and Means Committee.

Thus Ways and Means Democrats no longer reflected the old power structure of the House, which had been "the real power for the Committee," according to Conable, "because it meant that there was a presumption in favor of what the Ways and Means Committee brought to the floor. We could sustain a closed rule and also be assured that no junior, untried members would be appointed to our committee."

## Mills Resigns and an Era Ends

Wilbur Mills resigned in 1975, and was succeeded by Al Ullman of Oregon, a weaker and less effective chairman. An era had ended. "Ullman just was not able to assert the kind of leadership that Mills could," says Wayne Thevenot, "partly because he doesn't have Wilbur Mills' charismatic personality and partly because he lacks Mills' thorough knowledge of the tax laws. But not even Mills could have run Ways and Means as he did in the past because the situation has changed, not just in Ways and Means but in the House."

"Ullman had the disadvantage of coming in at a time when the committee had been terribly expanded and seniority had weakened," says Dan Thomasson. "He had none of the clout that Mills had and he couldn't control the committee like Wilbur could. There are certain committees that need to be tightly controlled. You can't write tax legislation with three hundred fifty guys! You can't have a Ways and Means Committee that has eighty members—how are you going to get anything done? Now that Mills has left and the committee has expanded, chaos has been reigning for at least a couple of years."

## Ways and Means Today

Today, Ways and Means has thirty-five members, a Democratic ratio of 23:12, six subcommittees, and Dan Rostenkowski of Illinois as chairman. "After the Democrats took away its political function," says Barber Conable, "they decided that in order to get a handle on the committee they should select people who would be responsive to the Caucus. So, a whole series of docile, untried, freshman Democrats were put on, which is a deliberate policy of Danny Rostenkowski. He said that if he were going to be chairman he wanted to have absolute control—he's from Chicago and the function of politics in Chicago is control. So, first of all Tip O'Neill agreed to stack the committee 23 to 12, even though that wasn't the ratio of the parties in the House, and to let Danny veto any new people going on which allowed Danny to choose those he knew he could control. Since Ways and Means was becoming a legislative committee and not a political power the senior members no longer cared about getting on it. After all, it's a pain in the neck. You have to deal with contentious issues—taxation is controversial—and you have to work too hard."

What other changes have there been since Mills' departure and the weakening of the seniority system? "I remember going in the committee room one time for an important tax hearing after Mills had resigned," recalls Thomasson, "and realizing that the committee had expanded, maybe doubled, its size. The members were in there shooting rubber bands at one another. That's how silly it was. This was after Mills had left, of course, but I'm sure he couldn't have controlled it anyway. Things are not quite the same."

Ways and Means was a great committee in those days.
—Paul Duke, congressional correspondent

## Notes

1. At that time it was composed of one House member from each state.
2. See Allen Schick, "The Three-Ring Budget Process: The Appropria-

tions, Tax, and Budget Committees in Congress," in Mann and Ornstein, *The New Congress*, p. 304–311.

3. See John E. Manley, "Wilbur D. Mills: A Study in Congressional Influence," in *The American Political Science Review*, vol. 63 (June 1969), p. 442.

4. Described in chapter 1.

5. See in chapter 1.

# 8

# The Small Empires: Seniority and the Growth of Subcommittees

The first thing I'd do is abolish all the subcommittees.
                                    —Former Senator Gale McGee

"I know not how better to describe our form of government in a single phrase than by calling it a government by the chairmen of the standing committees of Congress," wrote Woodrow Wilson in 1885. And, until nearly a century later when subcommittees began to assume a dominant role in the legislative process, the authority of committee chairmen remained unchallenged.

As the seniority system continued to weaken in the early 1970s, the power and the number of subcommittees began to increase, and by 1975 there were 268 subcommittees in both houses of Congress,[1] an addition of five over the year before.[2] Even with calls for cutbacks and the adoption of reform measures, the number stood at 214 in 1984.

As the number of subcommittees increased, their chairmen became more participatory, hiring their own staffs, and, some say, becoming as powerful as full committee chairmen.[3] Every Democratic Senator was a subcommittee chairman by the mid-1970s and in 1981 when the Republicans became the majority party in the Senate, each Republican Senator was assigned a subcommittee chairmanship. "Now any young hotshot who arrives in the House or the Senate—particularly in the Senate—is liable to have hurt feelings if he's not made chairman of a subcommittee within a couple of years," explains Bob Clark.

"The one advantage of numerous subcommittees," notes Samuel

Shaffer, "is that it gives a lot of Congressmen a 'piece of the action,' and satisfies their egos. The proliferation of subcommittees evolved from changes in the rules that relaxed the seniority system, and diluted the power of the full committee chairmen."

How has the increase of subcommittees affected the legislative process, the Congress—and even more importantly for the supporters of the seniority system—the full committee chairmen?[4]

"It's good," says Charles Ferris. "It's a way of ventilating the energies of the individual members. Everyone loves to have a problem to work on and giving everyone a subcommittee so he can work on something is good. You have interesting people with lots of energy and experience to bring to bear on problems, and you let their energy go and find a focus. It's healthy."

"The subcommittee system allows individual pieces of legislation, individual measures which require a certain amount of expertise, to get that full measure of expertise within the committee structure," says Anthony Zagami, counsel to the Joint Committee on Printing. "A piece of legislation can't become completely lost because it will have the individual attention of a subcommittee."

### Too Many Subcommittees

However, Clark, Ferris, and Zagami are in the minority. Even a former subcommittee chairman thinks there are too many. "The number of subcommittees should be reduced," says Paul Rogers, who used to chair the House Subcommittee on Health, "and consolidated as well. *Ad hoc* committees have been set up which really are doing oversight work that could and should be done by the legislative committees if they are properly organized and if they didn't have too much on their agendas." Another problem he sees is that "committees now are established for any subject that is popular for the moment, such as the Select Committee on Drugs. The Select Committee on Aging is another. It's a very large subcommittee, even though it doesn't have the authority to do anything except oversight. It's a ponderous machinery with a huge staff."

"Subcommittees should be cut back. There are far too many of them," said Frank Church. "This has not only interfered with the efficiency of Congress and added to its cost, it has made the process even more cumbersome than it was before. Also it has diffused the power within the Congress to the point of anarchy."

"There are so many subcommittees that there's not enough legislation for all to handle," says former Democratic Congressman Joseph Karth of Minnesota. "They start investigating things—including each other—and they're so busy with this that they don't have time to legislate."

"Scams!" says Nicholas Miller. "The proliferation of subcommittees is what people talk about because that's the obvious institutional shift; but all the subcommittees were scams for Senators to hire staff. A huge bureaucracy was created that had to justify its existence; and as soon as that happened, the old traditional seniority system could not continue to function because there were so many people trying to find ways around it. As soon as everyone starts getting staff, the whole nature of the place changes. There's really not much you can do to control that."

"It just feeds on itself," says Dan Thomasson, "and gets bigger and bigger. That's how bureaucracy works anyway."

"Too many subcommittees give rise to too many hearings and too many votes because everybody has a subcommittee and wants to be active and do something," says Gaylord Nelson. "All these subcommittees may dilute the power of the full committee chairman, and that necessarily may not be good either. If there are too many subcommittees, you then have too many people who are members of those subcommittees because you have to staff them. Or else you get a subcommittee so small that it doesn't represent a cross section of the committee itself. We were supposed to stop the proliferation of subcommittees with the Stevenson Committee[5] of which I was a member, but the Steering Committee violated that right off the bat. If a Senator serves on several subcommittees and attends all the hearings and markup sessions scheduled it is impossible for him to do a considered job in dealing with legislation."

"I was lucky," says Eugene McCarthy, "because at that time two of my committees—the House Ways and Means and the Senate Finance Committees—operated without any subcommittees. The Ways and Means Committee might set up a subcommittee for a particular purpose; however, there was nothing that could be considered a going subcommittee. The same was true for the Senate

Foreign Relations Committee where I was chairman of the African Subcommittee—but that was just for trips. All basic staff requirements were handled by the full committee. This has changed. For example, amending the Constitution should be the business of the full Judiciary Committee, but Judiciary now has a subcommittee for constitutional amendments. The Constitution has been amended only half a dozen times in the past one hundred fifty years, but when Birch Bayh [D., Indiana] was chairman of that subcommittee they were amending the Constitution every year: 'When in doubt, amend the Constitution.' Part of that was because there was a sub-committee."

Hugh Scott also refers to the Senate Judiciary Committee, recalling that "when the Senate Judiciary Committee was expanding rapidly, getting bigger and more unwieldy, Senator John Tunney of California was pleading for a new subcommittee because he was the only member of the majority party who wasn't a subcommittee chairman. Judiciary Committee Chairman Jim Eastland asked Tunney what the new subcommittee would do. 'If you create this sub-committee,' Tunney replied, 'I'll find things for it to do.' "

"Someone on the rise wants his own little forum," says Bob Clark, "so you give him a subcommittee. The problem is that if you give somebody a subcommittee he's going to use it to hold hearings that, in many cases, should not be held."

"Ridiculous," says Tom Korologos. "This adds tremendously to the cost of what people pay for their government. You're creating another budget, another expenditure. Moreover, there's no way that a member can do a top-notch, super, thoroughly complete job on any one subcommittee because he's on too many of them. I think there are so many subcommittees because every [majority party] Senator has to brag that he's chairman of something; otherwise, his constituents will wonder why. This is unfortunate."

### Subcommittee Jurisdictions

While there is no agreement on whether the growth of subcommittees benefited or hurt the legislative process, most congressional observers agree that their jurisdictions must be restructured. "The desire to spread the action around has led to the creation

of subcommittees with unclear jurisdictional lines that add an unmanageable quality to the House," says Fred Wertheimer.

"It's not so much the proliferation of subcommittees that is the
problem," says Wilbur Mills, "but the need to restructure their
jurisdictions. For example, when [then President Jimmy] Carter
sent his message on energy to the Hill there were five committees
and a great number of subcommittees in the House that had to
pass judgment—which involved maybe two hundred Congressmen. That's entirely too many to ever get a consensus on anything." Mills recommends "going back to what we had. Legislation
would move faster, smoother. We're making all these mistakes now
and there's a danged bill every year to correct the bill passed the
year before."

"It's difficult to move matter through a committee if the legislation has to be carried, not by one subcommittee, but sometimes
several subcommittees, due to cross-jurisdictional claims," says Hugh
Scott. "For instance, in what has become the fashion of the day,
as soon as the energy issue moved into prominence a decade or so
ago, every committee had to have an energy subcommittee and
the principal committee even added 'energy' to its name.[6] Natural
resources is another one. Everybody had to have natural resources. There was a need for action on civil rights and every committee had to have a subcommittee on either civil rights or human
rights. Then some committees felt they had to have a consumer
relations subcommittee. The subcommittees were proliferating and
generally getting in each other's way, delaying action by the full
committee, and vastly increasing the budget it takes to operate the
Congress."

"Power has been diffused so that any major legislation typically
must be reviewed by two or three, sometimes five or six, different
committees," said Frank Church. "You not only increase the over-
head costs of the Congress, you slow down the legislative process,
and it's much more difficult to fix responsibility for legislation. The
situation led a Canadian ambassador to observe that when he first
came to Washington, he was told that if anyone said he made a
decision in this town he was lying, because no one knows for sure
where the decisions are actually made or who in the end makes
them."

## Effect of Subcommittees on Committee Chairmen

While it may seem that the increasing activity of subcommittees dilutes the power of seniority and the committee chairmen, not all agree that it does—and of those who do agree, there is no consensus on whether this is beneficial to the Congress.

"It has strengthened the power of the committee chairman because granting subcommittee chairmanships builds up support for him," says F. Nordy Hoffman, former Senate Sergeant at Arms. "The committee chairman remains the boss, but allowing others to have a sense of participation, he builds his power. The chairman becomes stronger not weaker. When you watch floor action you can see subcommittee chairmen going to their committee chairmen on legislative matters, even if their philosophies differ."

"I don't think subcommittees weaken the power of the chairman," says Anthony Zagami, "rather, I think they enhance his power because, for the most part, he appoints the subcommittee chairmen and any legislation that is reported out of a subcommittee must still go to the full committee. That is not to say that the chairman maintains the level of power he held in the late 1950s and early 1960s when there were fewer subcommittees. The virtually total authority and control held by the committee chairman has been lost; but, overall, I think it has made the system work a little better."

Senator Bob Packwood of Oregon was an example of a chairman with undiluted powers when he headed the Senate Commerce Committee from 1981 until 1985,[7] according to Patrick O'Donnell. "When Packwood was Commerce Committee chairman," O'Donnell explains, "he just took the major issues that came before the Commerce Committee and preempted them. He did it himself at the full committee level. However, there are subcommittee chairmen who strike out on their own and that doesn't bother me. I see that as being somewhat orderly. The subcommittee should be small and work in a specifically defined area so that it can get results much faster than the full committee. The subcommittee mechanism is a good one as long as you don't have too many."

Herb Jasper also talks about the Commerce Committee under Senator Packwood as one in which the chairman retained control over his subcommittees. "The staff of the Senate Communications

Subcommittee [of the Senate Commerce Committee] turned over substantially; and, at one point, Senator Packwood assigned two people from other subcommittee staffs to Communications Subcommittee work and didn't even mention it to Senator Barry Goldwater of Arizona, the subcommittee chairman. During a markup on the Communications bill, Goldwater, who had been a cosponsor of the bill, publicly disavowed it. He fought Packwood over the bill, saying that it should be referred back to his subcommittee because sufficient hearings had not been held. To illustrate how little impact he had on that legislation, he publicly stated that he had not even been introduced to his new staff."

"The chairman still retains power," says Morris Amitay. "He can arrange with the subcommittee chairman to get something out that is somewhere near what he wants so that it can be worked on in the full committee. I can't think of any instance where a subcommittee chairman blocked a serious legislative proposal of the chairman. Of course, in some instances, subcommittees do reduce the power of the committee chairman, but usually that is power that the chairman wants to give away to the subcommittee chairman in any case. In many instances, you'll notice that the committee chairman is an *ex officio* member of a subcommittee. But if he wants to spend a lot of time working on that subcommittee and he has staff loyal to him, he may be able still to run that subcommittee unofficially because they have to defer to him to some extent."

Subcommittee chairmen are only as powerful as the chairman lets them be, stresses William Hildenbrand. "Each subcommittee chairman still has a committee chairman above him and his power is limited by the dictates of the chairman," says Hildenbrand. "For instance, [former Senate Judiciary Committee Chairman] James O. Eastland jealously guarded legislation, not allowing controversial or important legislation to be handled by subcommittees. And [former Senate Labor Committee Chairman] Harrison A. Williams of New Jersey decided that a committee chairman should not head a subcommittee, so instead of referring important bills to a subcommittee he handled them in full committee."

"Senator Eastland allowed a limited diffusion of power in his Judiciary Committee when he established subcommittes," recalls Wayne Thevenot. "Yet, Eastland did this in an attempt to buy peace. A subcommittee chairmanship would be granted in exchange for which Eastland retained ultimate control over all legislation emerging from the Judiciary Committee. Eastland's system worked for a long time; but there were factors he could not control including the press, lobbyists and, finally, the minor empires each subcommittee came inevitably to represent. As the issues became bigger and bigger than Jim Eastland, and the media permitted a greater number of people to be informed on the issues, Eastland's control lessened."

"Subcommittees not only dilute the power of the chairman, in the House they dilute the power of the Speaker," says Eugene McCarthy. "The whole thing is scattered out. In the House, it has had the effect of increasing the power of the caucus, which is a rather dangerous power. In the Senate, however, there is not quite the same effect because Senate rules are implemented more loosely. In the House, giving more power to the caucus weakens the institutional structure and the multiplicity of subcommittees weakens the Speaker and causes chaos. All these subcommittee chairmen have to go looking for something to do, whether it's legislative action or some kind of oversight or supervisory function. They all build a constituency for their subcommittee and staff."

## The Growing Importance of Subcommittee Chairmen: Henry A. Waxman and the House Health Subcommittee

In 1979, four years after the nonendorsement of three committee chairmen due their positions by seniority signaled the beginning of the decline of the seniority system, three subcommittee chairmen were denied their logical seats. There were differences between the 1975 and 1979 challenges: In 1975 the three chairmen lost their seats amid charges that they had been autocratic leaders who denied junior members legislative participation, whereas the 1979 challenges did not involve sitting chairmen. However, the successful challenges in 1979 by three Congressmen against more senior members dramatically points out the growing recognition of, and desire for, the power now held by subcommittee chairmen and the decline of the seniority system.

The most publicized struggle was for the chairmanship of the House Interstate and Foreign Commerce Committee's Health Subcommittee. Henry A. Waxman (D., California) won a victory over Richardson Preyer (D., North Carolina) who ranked three slots ahead of him in seniority on the full committee. The other two fights involved Bob Eckhardt (D., Texas) who defeated John M. Murphy (D., New York) for chairman of the Oversight and Investigations Subcommittee of the House Commerce Committee, and Toby Moffet (D., Connecticut) who won the chairmanship of the Government Operations Committee's Environment, Energy, and Natural Resources Subcommittee from three more senior members.

The chairmanship of the House Health Subcommittee became available with the retirement of Congressman Paul Rogers after twenty-four years in Congress. The Health Subcommittee was to be very active in 1979 because much legislation under its jurisdiction—including clean air programs, national health insurance, hospital construction, medical research, and prepaid health plans—was expected to come before Congress that year. Thus, the health panel was considered a very powerful subcommittee.

If the vacancy had occurred prior to the 1970s, the chair most likely would have passed to the Democratic member with the most years of consecutive subcommittee service, Congressman David E. Satterfield, III, of Virginia. But the "nondescript Virginian," as the *Chicago Tribune* called him, was not supported by his colleagues. He withdrew, thus placing Richardson Preyer, a moderate North Carolina Democrat, next in line. Preyer, a five-term Congressman, was highly respected, but the prospect of his assuming the chairmanship raised some serious questions.

Many elements of typical Washington political drama—charges of conflict of interest, unethical campaign contributions, and in this case, the Surgeon General's controversial report linking smoking to health problems, were to surface and contribute to the defeat of the member due the subcommittee chairmanship by seniority. Charges of conflict of interest were directed at millionaire Preyer, who had vast holdings in two large pharmaceutical firms, Richardson-Merrell and Sterling Drug., Inc. Should a chairman, it was asked, preside over legislation affecting the drug industry while he owned stock in pharmaceutical companies? In his defense, Preyer pointed out that all his assets were placed in a blind trust and he had refrained from voting on all drug-related matters during his subcommittee tenure. Moreover, Preyer promised, he would abstain from considering any measure regulating the industry. This statement, naturally, brought the charge that his effectiveness as a chairman would be reduced. "It is a tough problem," he conceded at the time, but insisted it would not make him a "one-legged chairman." His position was considered inadequate by several liberal interest groups because many issues peripherally related to the drug industry, such as national health insurance and Medicaid drug payments, were expected to be on the subcommittee's agenda that session. "I feel I can be fair and objective," Preyer said a few weeks before the House Caucus met to vote, countering the charge of "gross conflict" from Sidney Wolfe of the public advocacy Health Research Group who, at the same time, praised Waxman as "excellent."

Charges of unethical campaign contributions were leveled at Waxman. He had established a political action committee and donated $24,000 in campaign funds to ten members of the House Interstate and Foreign Commerce Committee, the parent committee to the Health Subcommittee, and an additional $21,000 to thirty other members of the House and Senate. These contributions, while unusual from a junior member, did not violate any law; however, the *New York Times* commented that they produced "a strong odor."

"What's wrong with a man helping out his colleagues?" Waxman protested, denying he was trying to enhance his chances of becoming chairman. Rather, he explained, he was helping "deserving progressives" retain their seats. He had received more money from his wealthy supporters than he needed, he said, and "was pleased to be able to help in some small way those poeple whose views I shared."

The attention swung back to Preyer. The Surgeon General released a new report affirming the earlier findings linking smoking to health problems, and prompting Preyer to react as would be expected by a Congressman representing a tobacco-producing state. Denouncing the report as based on "statistics rather than on solid research," Preyer called for an independent body, other than the Department of Health, Education and Welfare[8] to study the matter. Preyer's attack on the report brought immediate public opposition from several health groups. "Pro-tobacco," charged American Cancer Society official Allan K. Jonas, who expressed "profound misgivings" about Preyer. The press joined in as well. The *Wash-*

*ington Post*, which had previously endorsed Preyer for the chairmanship, editorialized that it "was moved to second thoughts" about his candidacy.

Commerce Committee Democrats met and voted by secret ballot on January 30. First, they voted yes or no on Preyer to head the health panel and he lost, 12–15. Waxman then bid for the post, seniority having been set aside, and won by a vote of 21–6. After the lopsided decision, Preyer denied that "the more peripheral" issues—the drug company holdings and the Surgeon General's report—determined the outcome. The deciding factors, Preyer said, were "generational and philosophical. It boiled down to the young liberals versus older moderates." What was significant, he said, was "the erosion of the seniority system." Also significant was the recognition of the importance of a subcommittee chairmanship.

> Subcommittees may be a hindrance to the legislative process, but they're important to the egos of their chairmen.
> —Former Congressman Frank Ikard

### Notes

1. 126 in the Senate and 142 in the House.
2. Four more in the House and one more in the Senate.
3. See Roger H. Davidson, "Subcommittee Government: New Channels for Policy Making," in Mann and Ornstein, *The New Congress*, p. 100–133.
4. See Christopher J. Deering and Steven S. Smith, "Subcommittees in Congress," in *Congress Reconsidered*, pp. 189–210.
5. In 1977, the Senate Resolution 4, the Stevenson Resolution, named after Senator Adlai Stevenson, III (D., Illinois), limited the number of committees on which a Senator may serve. It also put a ceiling on the number of chairmanships members may maintain: Membership was limited to three committees and eight subcommittees; chairmanships were limited to a maximum of three committees and subcommittees combined.
6. The Senate Energy and Natural Resources Committee was formerly the Interior and Insular Affairs Committee, and the House Energy and Commerce Committee had been the Interstate and Foreign Commerce Committee.
7. Senator Packwood is currently chairman of Senate Finance.
8. Now known as the Department of Health and Human Services.

# 9

# A Multiplicity of Authorities: Staff, Support, and Seniority

It is rather asinine for the Congress to appropriate millions of dollars, yes, even billions of dollars for the staffing of the executive branch of the government with lawyers, statisticians, engineers, and economists, and fail to have the courage to set up a similar body for themselves and to appropriate ample funds for obtaining the best impartial body of experts in America upon any and all legislative subjects.

—Congressman Charles M. LaFollette
(R., Indiana), 1943

Twenty years after Congressman LaFollette made the above statement 6,000 persons were on the congressional payroll. And twenty years after that, the number topped 31,000, 7,500 of whom worked directly for members of Congress.[1] "However," points out Dan Thomasson, "we still have the same number of Congressmen!"

Although congressional employees—the invisible, influential, nonelected policy-making subpopulation of Capitol Hill—are not directly affected by the seniority system, indirectly they are very definitely a factor in the congressional power structure. As a member of Congress rises in power, he can hire more employees; but, it should be recognized, it is also possible that the more employees a member has, the more they control the member—a not infrequent occurence. Either way, two things are sure: Congressional staff has grown spectacularly and this growth has had a great impact on the balance of power.[2]

"Congressional staff has become an enormous bureaucracy," Dan

Thomasson continues. "We used to talk about bureaucracy being a problem of the administrative branch, but now it's the same thing in Congress. Congress used to be the one place you could go to get relief from bureaucracy. Now they're empire builders, too. They build new buildings every five minutes and when you get new buildings, the bureaucracy grows in direct proportion to the amount of space it takes to fill it. That's all there is to it. If there's space available, you're going to have people there. It's absolutely ridiculous!"

But there are more legitimate reasons for the increase in staff.[3] "The growth in staff is partly a response to the increase in issues that must be handled by legislators," says Anthony Zagami. "In addition, with the growth of special interest groups and trade organizations there are increased questions that staff have to handle. This has to be done by someone; a member cannot do it alone. It's impossible." Zagami sees the growth of congressional staff as a result of the "increased awareness of the American public and its appetite for information and knowledge about what the Congress is doing." Don Phillips agrees with Zagami. "I don't think there's too much staff. People come to Congress for help and it's about time that Congress had the staff to do the job."

The amount of work handled by each member of Congress has increased dramatically during the past few decades.[4] "Members are overloaded," says Gaylord Nelson. "It began to change after the Second World War. Bob LaFollette, Wisconsin's Senator twenty years before me, was probably better staffed with three or four people than a member is nowadays with forty, because you weren't dealing with all the programs you deal with now. LaFollette would receive fifteen to eighteen letters a day—almost all from people he knew—and his secretary would drive to his home in Georgetown where he would dictate the answers. In contrast, by the end of my term in 1980, we were averaging about fifty letters an hour—that's four hundred a day! Well over one hundred thousand a year!"

"It's entirely different today," agrees Wilbur Mills. "When I first came to Congress in 1939, I'd be lucky to get three or four letters a day and maybe a call a week. You got homesick, actually, because nobody called you. But now! The more load you have, the more staff you need."

"When I came to Congress in 1949," recalls Eugene McCarthy,

"we had enough money to pay three people. You could stretch it out to handle four, if you wanted to, but it was barely enough for three. Today, if you just let it run wild, Congress could achieve a complete mirror duplication of the executive branch of government in every office. It's moving in that direction now."

## Staff Power

As the number of congressional employees has grown,[5] many contend that their power has increased as well, to the detriment both of the member served and the Congress as a whole. Members of Congress are elected, and staff is not. Thus the question arises: how much of the lawmaking process should be handled by staff? It should be remembered, however, that the amount of power delegated to an employee is determined by the member who hired the person.

"There's no question that as your staff gets bigger there's a real danger that, as a committee chairman, you can find yourself with staffers who write hearings the way they want to write them," says Marlow Cook.

William Hathaway says that "you can argue—quite reasonably—that you need all these staff people, because you need all this information to make an intelligent decision. But if the pace of legislation were slowed down, the member himself would have more time to study matters and wouldn't need as much staff. The shortcoming of having so much staff is that once a staff person gets a certain area of expertise, he is forever handing you a bunch of memos and saying that you ought to get into this and you ought to get into that. It extends the member's work day beyond the twenty-four hours that God has allotted and it wears him down."

"Actually," Hathaway continues, "on the Senate side, the staff runs a lot of the Senators. Some of the staffs get to feeling their oats and become sort of arrogant toward other members. The staff allowance could be cut down which would help considerably, because if you couldn't hire as many staff people you wouldn't have that much pressure put on you to do so. The legislative calendar could be slowed down and there would be more time for a member to think about things."

"The expansion of staff is ridiculous!" says Tracy Mullin. "There's too much staff, and the staff has too much power. Frequently the staff makes decisions about what bills the member will introduce and how those bills are written. It depends on the individual member, of course, and the staff person, but in many cases the member is nothing more than a mouthpiece."

Frank Church agreed that staff growth has been "a serious error." He said that "the theory that the Congress needs to be staffed like the executive branch in order to cope is very dubious. I can't see that such staffing has proved helpful to the Congress in its legislative function. I can see lots of evidence that it has had just the opposite impact. The staff feels obliged to recommend putting changes in the law, sort of speciality items. Each committee staffer has a little personal program and looks for a Senator on his committee to sponsor this little change or that little change. Members find themselves serving staff, and whatever creativity or imagination a Senator might bring to bear upon problems himself tends to be diluted by the time and attention given to staff recommendations. Time is a precious commodity in Congress. It's hard enough, under ideal circumstances, to find enough time to think about what your're doing, but the little time that you have for the purpose is often consumed by staffers importuning you to do this and do that. Members are functioning less as legislators than they did when they weren't overwhelmed by their own staffs."

"It's no trick to delegate a great deal of authority to your staff," points out Senator Proxmire. "You can delegate so much that you don't really do your job. I think that in some ways the reason why the Founding Fathers were so superior to those who followed them is because they had to do all their work—they didn't have anybody to write speeches or to explore issues for them. If the Congress or Senator didn't understand the issues himself, he was unable to function at all. Today you have a staff that will do a great deal of work for you; so it isn't always easy to know whether it's the Senator talking or the staff talking."

"I think we have become very wasteful as we build up congressional staffs," says Bob Clark. "Congress is going to have to start disciplining itself one of these days. Of course, there are a lot of very competent people working on the Hill and it's better to have your own experts than to rely on the executive branch." On the other hand, Clark says, increasing congressional staff is "only a good thing if you're giving no consideration at all to money, because it accounts for a lot of the taxpayers' money."

## Is Increased Staff Wasteful?

"The budget for the Congress is now over one billion dollars[6] and it used to be $100 million," says Dan Thomasson, "and I don't think the people are any better served with an increased budget. It's incredible what has happened to the Congress. The more people you put to work, the more things they're going to suggest. I don't think that's always very good. A bureaucrat will want to do something and it may not always be what you want him to do."

Duplication of work is another problem, complains Michael Pertschuk. "When there is too much staff, they tend to cancel each other out and make a lot of work for each other. Members tend to want their staffs to take initiatives, and the staff wants to build a legislative record for their members; so you get a great deal of overlapping and sometimes counterproductive efforts."

"I'm a strong believer that they should do something to get the staff situation under control," says Patrick O'Donnell. "Congressmen and Senators are being hit with memos and ideas by staff all the time. All these staffers are trying to justify their own existence. It becomes a neverending, always growing, circle of confusion. It has gotten out of hand. There are just too many."

"I think staffs will continue to increase," says Senator Proxmire. "You know what happens. We build more buildings so we can house more staff; then we get that housing we hire more staff. In addition to that we have a number of Senators—and I'm sure Congressmen—who have too many staff people working in their state. There is one Senator I know who has seven separate offices in his state. That's really absurd. The people out in the state just work full time on reelecting the Senator."

Wilbur Mills remembers Ray Madden, House Rules Committee chairman, protesting several years ago that each member of his committee wanted to hire a legislative assistant "I don't understand it, Wilbur," he said, "why does Rules need legislative assistants? The committee doesn't legislate." The assistants were hired.

If I get one more staffer, I'll have to put a padlock on my door.
—Former Senator John O. Pastore
(D., Rhode Island) as told to Patrick O'Donnell

## Notes

1. CBS News, "Sixty Minutes," October 16, 1983.

2. See Michael Malbin, "Delegation, Deliberation, and the New Role of Congressional Staff," in Mann and Ornstein, *The New Congress*, pp. 134–177.

3. Norman Ornstein, et al., *Vital Statistics on Congress*, pp. 116–137.

4. See Harrison W. Fox, Jr., and Susan Webb Hammond, *Congressional Staffs* (New York: The Free Press, 1977).

5. See Christopher Deering and Steven S. Smith, "Subcommittees in Congress," in *Congress Reconsidered*, pp. 198–9.

6. The budget for Congress in fiscal 1984 was $1,211,055,800; when supplementals were included, the total reached $1,284,019,800.

# 10

# Room for Improvement: Should Seniority Survive?

Always remember that Congress does two things well: nothing and overreact.

—Tom C. Korologos,
congressional lobbyist for President Nixon

As long as there has been a Congress, there have been recommendations for improving it. Yet changes have come slowly, the most inviolate rules not those mandated by the Constitution, but the ones derived from tradition and custom—and thus it has been with the seniority system. Tempering, if not entirely eliminating, abuses by autocratic committee chairmen has been the aim of most of the serious reform proposals that seek to replace seniority as the basis for the selection of chairmen. The method most often suggested, though never put into practice (except in special circumstances such as the House Budget and Senate Ethics committees), is rotation.

## Rotation of Chairmanships

With a few variables, all proposals for rotation of chairmanships fall into two distinct categories: (1) rotation of the chair among all majority members of each committee (applicable to both houses), and (2) rotating each committee's chair among all majority members of the entire body (limited to the Senate because of its smaller size).

The strongest argument in favor of limiting a chairman's tenure is that it would democratize the Congress, curbing potential abuses through a diffusion of power. A chairman "would be prevented from developing an empire, a fiefdom," says Patrick O'Donnell.

Gaylord Nelson would impose a limit on a chairman's length of service. "A period could be picked, say, six or eight years, for a chairman's tenure," says Nelson, "then the next one in seniority from the same party would become the chairman unless he's rejected by the caucus. The previous chairman would be eligible again at some later date. I feel that if a former chairman has a lot of support he could become chairman again the following session. That's about the only suggestion I ever thought of that would be practical; yet I'm not absolutely sure how valuable that would be."

Senator Bumpers agrees that "if committees elected their chairmen every two to four years it would have a very salutory effect on the chairman's conduct. It would make him more responsive. I'm not sure about how often to hold committee elections. I once suggested every six years, but perhaps every four years would be better, and I'm not saying that two could be wrong. I would allow each committee to choose its chairman, with the assignments still given by the Steering Committee."

Former Senator Abourezk would replace seniority with "a merit system, by which I mean that committees would vote for their chairman. There's nothing wrong with that. Obviously it's going to be a member of the majority, but, amongst them, the members of the majority party ought to vote every two years. If you want to retain the seniority system, then limit the chairman to a two-year term, after which he goes to the bottom of the seniority ladder. There would be a real rotation system, an automatic rotation."

Rotating chairmanships of all committees among the majority members of the Senate has few supporters. "It wouldn't work," says Tracy Mullin. "Some issues are not commensurate with some states' needs. Senators do have the right to pick a field in which they have some background and knowledge. Members should be matched up with interest areas."

In fact, most congressional observers come down against both proposals. "If you rotate chairmanships," says Morris Amitay, "you completely diffuse the power of the chairman. Do you want to do that? You just create more independence and more anarchy. It could become really unmanageable. I think you're better off to have at least one focal point."

Rampant anarchy and chaos throughout the legislative process is the result most feared from rotation. Coming a close second is the loss of expertise that a chairman has gained by long involvement with a committee's subject matter. "It would knock down the quality of expertise," says Wilbur Mills. "I feel sorry for the members now. They just don't have the time to study legislation."

"Expertise? What expertise does one need in the Senate or the House?" asks James Abourezk. "The real requirement is the ability to make political decisions and if you've gone through a campaign you've learned how to make those. Besides the staff has great expertise. All a member needs to know when he comes to Congress is how to locate the men's or lady's room in the Capitol."

Gaylord Nelson disagrees and says that rotating the chair at the beginning of each new Congress "would not be good because it's an awfully short time for a chairman really to master the job. On some occasions you could end up with a newly elected member going on a committee and immediately being made the chairman which would create a lot of complications in managing legislation."

"There has to be some continuity in the life of a committee," says Anthony Zagami, "both at the level of the chairman and the level of staff. When you change the leadership on a constant basis, many people don't realize that, more than likely, it necessitates a change of senior staff. That would put a great damper on the progress that a committee is able to make. One of the key factors in any committee's work is the staff that supports the members. You have to have a staff that is well informed, that has developed a fair amount of expertise in the subject matter, and is familiar with the way the legislative process works. It takes quite some time to get familiarized with the workings of a committee and to understand how it operates and fits into the overall scheme. And that's only one good reason for stability."

A modification of the rotation method which would allow for the accrual of expertise while diminishing the possibility of an autocratic hold by one person would be to rotate the chairmanship within each committee but to make it a "step" rotation. This proposal, offered by George Herman, would use the "escalator system" by which the vice-chairman becomes the chairman and another member moves to the vice-chairman position. "The vice-chairman would have to do a lot of work," says Herman, "and by the time he became chairman he would have had some experience."

"It would be more confusing than ever," disagrees Dan Thomasson. "The committee would still not have a permanent head who had continuity through a number of years and who could say which way the committee was going." Countering the argument that a strong committee chairman could refuse to report out legislation supported by a majority of his committee, Thomasson says that "there are devices for getting legislation out of committee when there's a reluctant chairman." While he admits that members are reluctant to use discharge positions, he still comes down against the rotation of committee chairs because "it would just make it even more chaotic."

The consensus is that for all the aforementioned reasons—and particularly for the stability that seniority offers—rotating chairmanships would be an undesirable, and probably unworkable, method of selecting chairmen.

Only the newest members would support a rotation system, points out William Hildenbrand. "Most likely," he says, "a 'new breed' entering the Senate would rather see a rotation system and a move away from seniority; but, after they have served one term and begun to accumulate seniority, they don't want to lose it."

### Placing Age and Service Limitation

Limiting the number of terms served or setting a maximum age for members of Congress would also restrict the amount of power a chairman could accrue by denying him open-ended tenure. The Constitution sets a minimum age of eligibility—twenty-five for the House and thirty for the Senate—but no maximum; and the number of terms a member can serve is left to the discretion of the voters. Senator McClure, against setting a maximum age limit, believes that "Congress needs a mixture of age and experience combined with youthful exuberance." He illustrates his position by recounting a discussion he had a few years ago: "I was sitting next to George Miller of Georgia, chairman of the House Committee on Science and Astronautics—that's now the Committee on Science and Technology—on a plane to Antarctica. That takes thirteen hours and there's time to discuss lots of things. George Miller and I were talking about something, when John Wold of Wyoming, one of the younger members and a geological engineer with a finely trained scientific mind, said 'We ought to do such and such.' George replied, 'We tried that fifteen years ago and it didn't work.' We need that kind of perspective, a combination of experience and institutional memory. That is important. That John Wold could challenge Miller could mean that perhaps the proposal's time has come. You need both sides. You only get that diversity of age and experience if you do not have artificial limitations. There shouldn't be an age limit in the law because the voters take care of whether a guy has been around too long."

"An old greezer falling asleep during a committee hearing is not helpful—and that has happened," says former Republican Congresswoman Millicent Fenwick of New Jersey. "Oddly enough, it happens when the chairman is the most loved and the most respected. Then people don't like to hurt his feelings until it becomes absolutely essential to do something for the welfare of the committee."

Gale McGee agrees that "age isn't really the important factor; it is cumulative experience that produces a mature judgment." McGee leans toward the Chinese custom of venerating the wisdom of age. "Even though it's sometimes abused, that's far less serious than shortchanging ourselves by losing that accumulated judgment," he concludes.

Some of the greatest leaders the world has ever known—Adenauer, Churchill, de Gaulle, Gandhi—have been up in their years, reflects Dale Bumpers, but he recognizes that "a lot of people get senile and ought not to go on serving. Nevertheless, to say that we ought to put an age limit might have deprived us of some of the greatest minds that ever served here." He concludes that as time goes by his "horizons on what is old changes."

Haynes Johnson used to favor an age limit of seventy for Senators and Congressmen, but now he is "much more reluctant to put on any limitation. I would make the case that if you look over the last generation you would see that some of the best people were driven for one reason or another out of the system. They don't last very long." On the other hand, Johnson concludes, a compulsory retirement age of seventy "makes lots of sense and it works elsewhere in our society."

Gale McGee opposes limiting the number of terms. He feels

that the reason for such a proposal is to "find a short cut to change the parliamentary body. It's like the proposal the New Dealers put forth to enlarge the Supreme Court when it was knocking down Roosevelt's legislation. [Limiting terms] would be an institutional change, dictated by the emotion of the moment, rather than a procedural change in the interests of government."

Senator Bumpers also is opposed to limiting the number of House and Senate terms. "There is a trade off. If you choose seniority, some people do indeed get too old, get senile, and ought to leave. If there were a limit of, say, three terms, a lot of people simply would not be allowed to reach that stage. Also it would prevent people from getting a bad case of 'Potomac fever,' and wanting to stay here forever. If they knew they could stay only two or three terms, perhaps they would conduct themselves in a more statesmanlike manner and not play politics quite so much. On the other hand, a limitation would insult the electorate and its intelligence. If the people of a particular state want to elect somebody five or six times that should be their prerogative. For us to pass a law saying that they are not smart enough to know whether a person ought to serve five terms or not would take away that prerogative. It would be an insult to the people and is alien to the representative process."

"If I could change Congress," says Patrick O'Donnell, "I would limit the number of terms a member could serve to two terms for the Senate, and perhaps four for the House—something like that— twelve years and eight years, respectively. That's arbitrary, but it should be something less than a lifetime in Congress, yet long enough to be there and make their marks. They could go out for a session and then come back and run again if they wanted to. There should be more rotation because these guys get too powerful, and forget where they came from. They begin to think they're special and believe their own press releases, think they're named for greatness. Too many of these guys in Congress get too powerful and they don't want to leave. A limit on the number of terms would be the best thing because they would be forced to go out and work in the marketplace. Let new guys come in and stay for no longer than eight years or so. And then get the hell out."

"Senators should be elected for no more than two terms," says Tracy Mullin, "and there should be a limit in the House, too. The staff people and the agencies would provide continuity. On the other hand, this would mean members would be desperately trying to make their marks on history quickly, and a lot of legislation would be rushed through."

## Strengthen Party Leadership

William Hathaway recommends that the party caucuses be strengthened "to shift power from committee chairmen to the party leadership, which would allow us to exert some discipline with respect to the amount of legislation. Various bills could be hashed out in the caucuses and firm decisions could be made on party positions." Although he would like the party caucuses to play a bigger role, he doesn't foresee that happening. If it did, "we would be more like a parliamentary form of government in which Cabinet members suggest legislation."

Alan Boyd also would like to see stronger party discipline because it is "quite important for party health and party health is a very important thing in this country. I sort of yearn for a parliamentary system like that in Britain, so we know where everybody stands. We have reached a stage in America where nobody is responsible for anything. In our system, unlike the British parliamentary system, there's no way to say, 'This is what they said they were going to do; this is what they did; and this is how they explained the difference.' I think party discipline is important, but I don't know how we're going to get back to it. That was one of the things that was weakened by the congressional reforms."

Senator Proxmire disagrees and believes in "very undisciplined parties in which members are free to make up their own minds on the issues. Things can function pretty well on that basis." However, Proxmire thinks that "it would be a good idea for the party to take positions and to have the members stand up and be counted on them. I mean you wouldn't have to support your party position—you could depart from it—but a party position would be helpful for members making decisions."

## Restructuring the Subcommittee System

Recommendations to cut back the number of subcommittees[1] are designed to reverse, or at least limit, dispersion of authority.[2]

Although these proposals would not directly limit the power of subcommittee chairmen, there would, at least, be fewer of them.

Senator McClure suggests not only reducing the number of committee and subcommittee assignments but strengthening the requirements for members to attend and participate. "The committee is where the work is done, yet we're spread too thinly. We cannot do the work in the committee. We must reduce the areas of responsibility, and at the same time require members to be more responsible. How you accomplish the latter is a little more difficult because there must either be an authority that can discipline or an external political force that can make a difference. There's no real discipline about whether a member attends a committee or not; he can be a member and never show up. I think the voting percentage on the floor is a very inaccurate measure of whether a person is working effectively. It is really a matter of time management. There should be times of the year set aside for committee work and there should be a way of requiring that members be there working and not off doing something else."

Senator Proxmire points out that it would be very difficult to reduce the number of subcommittees because every majority party Senator wants to have at least one subcommittee chairmanship. "It might be a little neater on paper to have far fewer subcommittees, and you might get better attendance at the meetings," he says, "but I'm not sure better legislation would result. I think the best we can expect is to have a majority of committee members at the markups."

Gale McGee would abolish all subcommittees and start over again. "It's unconscionable!" he says. "A Senator cannot attend all those subcommittee meetings. Besides many of them were created just to give another member of whichever party a chairmanship so he could say he was a chairman. In too many cases they invent a subcommittee just to give somebody something to do. It's ridiculous."

Dan Thomasson agrees that the number of subcommittees should be cut because "you don't have to have a subcommittee for every little thing. That's crazy and it just increases the special interests' influence. Those with no special interests except the economy and their own pocketbooks lose out."

In addition to reducing the number of subcommittees, many

congressional observers also recommend redefining or restructuring their jurisdictions. Melvin Laird points out that the Defense
Department can "play" eight committees against each other."If you
lose in one," he says, "you go to another; if you lose in another,
you can go to still another. You trade around. If you lose in one
but win in another, you can use that one. They're all scattered.
Committee and subcommittee jurisdictions must be redefined."

Alan Boyd remembers participating, as Transportation Secretary, with the General Accounting Office in the early 1970s on a
transportation study. At that time he counted twenty-eight
congressional committees or subcommittees that dealt with transportation, making development of a national transportation policy
impossible. "The various committees were not looking at the overall transportation system or the federal role in it," he recalls. "Rather
each looked at the one segment under its jurisdiction as if it were
the whole system. This has been improved to a substantial degree
because much of the transportation legislation now goes to the House
Public Works Committee rather than the old House Interstate and
Foreign Commerce Committee, but there is still a ways to go."

### Reform the Reforms

Wilbur Mills says, "I'd undo a lot of what we have done. I voted
for everything that happened so it's as much my vote as anybody's.
I would undo everything we started doing in the 1960s. I wouldn't
have open committee sessions, though I would allow the press to
cover them. I just would not permit the lobbyists and the public
to attend. It was claimed that the public wanted to see our committee sessions, that they had a right to know, but the public isn't
interested. They don't come. Instead the rooms are full of lobbyists. Also I would make some changes in the subcommittees, not
abolishing them, but somehow improving the system. The process
is too slow. To sum up, I would recommend going back as much
as possible to the pre-1960 rules. We shouldn't try to figure out
how to change; rather we should try to figure out what's wrong
with the present system and get rid of the 'improvement.' "

My thought is that it's going to be a long time before all these frailties and flaws in our system are going to be rectified to any degree at all.

—Senator James A. McClure

## Notes

1. Addressed in Chapter 8.

2. Christopher J. Deering and Steven S. Smith, "Subcommittees in Congress," in *Congress Reconsidered*, pp. 199–209.

# 11

# Epilogue:
# The Future of Seniority

The Senate has managed from roughly 1970 or 1971 onward to so
pervert and torture the processes of this body that we are approaching being inert.

—Senator Bob Packwood

The reform movement never dies in the Congress; rather it is
shunted aside for other, more politically appealing matters. During
the second session of the 98th Congress, it was revived again, pushed
to the forefront by the freshman Republican Senator from Indiana,
Dan Quayle, chairman of the Temporary Select Committee to Study
the Senate Committee System.

The mandate of the Quayle Committee[1] is to conduct a thorough
study of the Senate committee system, including the structure,
jurisdiction, number, and optimum size of Senate committees; the
number of subcommittees; committee rules and procedures; media
coverage of meetings; staffing and other committee facilities. The
Temporary Committee disbanded sixty days after issuing its report, in line with Senator Quayle's stated position on reducing the
number of committees.

Quayle kept to his promise that his committee's report would
contain recommendations on the most effective methods of committee oversight of federal programs, consistent procedures for the
referral of legislation, and workable methods of review and revi-
sion of committee jurisdictions.

Shortly before the committee's two days of hearings on July 31
and August 2, 1984, Senator Quayle took the floor and asked his

colleagues to appear before his committee and join him in a "process of institutional reflection." He called for an end to the "trivialization" of the Senate's work and to the "proliferation" of Senate committees and subcommittees, personal committee staff, floor amendments, cloture votes, and fiscal processes.

Senator Quayle told his colleagues on the Senate floor: "If the Senate is to retain its rightful place as the premier institution in public policy formulation . . . it must reform not only its committee system but also many of its rules and procedures. . . . We are doing a lot of things, but not very well and we are hardly doing anything well. We are not setting national priorities. We are not focusing our attention on crucial issues.

"No individual Senator can be expected to give up the rights and advantages that he has under our rules and customs unless we all do. . . . Individual self-restraint cannot deal with this problem. What we need is collective self-restraint. It is my hope that the Temporary Select Committee on Committees can make recommendations that will make it easier for us to engage in that collective self-restraint which I believe is essential to return the Senate to its proper functioning as the world's greatest political institution, an institution that will debate the issues, discuss the facts, formulate opinions, and establish public policy that will lead this nation. . . .

"We must chart some different procedures if we want to maintain reverence for this institution in the formulation of the national public policy. To continue the status quo, in my opinion, will enhance the trivialization of the Senate into a lesser power than it has been or it deserves. For the Senate to do better, we must be willing as individuals to do better for the sake of the institution."[2]

Quayle's goals sound noble, but reform and efficiency also can mean loss of independence and power for individual Senators. If the number of subcommittees is reduced, so are the number of chairmanships; and if floor procedure becomes more efficient, that could mean the restriction of unlimited debate—considered by some a cherished right and others an abused privilege.

The Temporary Select Committee's hearings focused on

- the budget process
- relationship of authorizations and appropriations

- committee assignment limitations, committee rules, scheduling, jurisdiction, and staffing
- creating, merging, or abolishing committees
- Senate floor procedure
- Senate schedule and agenda

Much of the hearing was devoted to simplifying the three-tiered budget–authorization–appropriations process and extending the one-year budget cycle to two years.[3] However, the Senate is known to cling to tradition, even if the result is inefficiency. The separate authorizations and appropriations processes have been with us since the 19th century, and the Budget Act—enacted in the mid-1970s to help Congress deal with totals and to establish priorities—was not accepted easily. However, Congress has not been able to meet its one-year fiscal deadlines—not for appropriations or authorizations or for the budget—which instigated the most recent call for simplification and for more time.

While no agreement could be reached on a specific method of amending the budget procedure, there was overwhelming support for changing it. Many proposals were offered, including: making the budget cycle biennial, enforcing current budget deadlines, changing the membership of the Budget Committee, and eliminating both the process and the Budget Committee itself. Other recommendations called for changing the length of the authorization and appropriations cycles and combining or more distinctly separating the authorizations and appropriations functions.

There also was support for imposing limitations on the number of committee and subcommittee assignments for each Senator, restricting or abolishing proxy votes in committee, publishing all committee votes, and holding joint House and Senate hearings when Cabinet members testify. Support was voiced also for scheduling committee hearings more efficiently and holding more hearings outside of Washington. In addition, testimony was offered recommending the realignment of committee jurisdictions, reducing the number of staff, and reducing the number of committees by merging two or more committees or subcommittees.

Proposals for changing floor procedure were offered as well. These included enforcing the germaneness rule, prohibiting unwritten amendments, modifying the cloture rule, requiring a floor schedule, restricting the number of committee staff allowed on the floor, and shortening the congressional session, the workweek structure, or modification of both.

Senator Quayle declared that his hearings had two main objectives: to explore the problems of committee and subcommittee proliferation and assignment limitations, and to find ways to streamline the budget–authorization–appropriations process in order to reduce "perceived redundancies."[4] The committee's co-chairman, Democratic Senator Wendell Ford of Kentucky, however, urged caution. Unless the present system of committee organization and operation is clearly defective, he said, the committee should not recommend changing it. He also pointed out that if the Senate work load is too great, corrective action must be directed at that problem, not at the organizational system.

Howard Baker, the Senate Majority Leader at the time, was the lead-off witness. Baker, a frequent critic of current Senate procedure, discussed the relationship of the committee system to the Senate itself. "I am often distressed," he told the committee, "to find an attitude that almost amounts to a statement of first loyalty and first dedication to the committee assignment, rather than the Senate on behalf of Senators." Baker's point was that the important work of the Congress is handled in committees rather than on the Senate floor, causing the Senate to forfeit "a great amount of its status as the nation's prime forum for the debate of public issues."[5] He also called for a lessening of the Senate work load.

Baker said that the Senate majority and minority leaders should not be given committee assignments— "a waste of time," he called it—because of the great amount of time they spend running the Senate. "I would propose," Baker told the committee, "that the two leaders should not be members of any committees but, rather, should be *ex officio* members of all committees and free to attend and participate in the deliberations of all committees, not to vote, however." Baker also took the opportunity to state again his concept of the "citizen legislator"[6] calling for shorter congressional sessions and more hearings outside of Washington.

Turning to what he termed the "three-layer cake" of authorizations, appropriations, and budget, Baker said that the committee's first responsibiity should be to simplify the procedure. Baker suggested a two-year authorization cycle and annual appropriations to "set out basic objectives and goals." He said he would support a two-year budget— "two budget resolutions is mind-boggling"—and the combining of some authorizations and appropriations functions.

Countering the argument that the three-pronged budget authorizations appropriations process should be restricted, Senate Budget Chairman, Republican Pete Domenici of New Mexico, called for the creation of a joint House–Senate Budget Committee. He said that stricter controls on the budget process are more likely to ease the work load of the Senate than consolidating one or more of the three committees. Domenici also said that more attention should be focused on insuring that each step in the process acccomplishes its original purpose. "We have frequently used the appropriations process to debate substantive policy issues," he told the committee, "and the result has often been delay." He pointed out that Congress has completed more appropriations bills annually since the Budget Committee was created in 1974 than it had before it was established.

Domenici contended that "the inability of authorizations to be done on time is not the fault of any process. It simply means that in a time of moving away from the almost impulsive legislative activism of the 1960s and 1970s toward a more cautious legislative behavior, consensus has often been hard to achieve." Domenici pointed out that one of the reasons for the slower pace in the Senate is the historical difference between the operation of the two houses of Congress. "We have consciously chosen, from Constitutional days, to make the Senate the deliberative body," he said, referring to the Senate's unlimited debate and comparing it to the House's "more streamlined character." Avoiding error, he said, is more important than creating efficiency.

A joint House–Senate Budget Committee, Domenici assured the committee, would be one way to improve efficiency because the budget process could be speeded up if the same resolution was reported to both houses, and it would be easier to work out differences after floor action. He also proposed that the leaders of the two houses be represented on the Joint Committee.

Opposing Domenici's views was retiring Republican Senator John Tower of Texas who said that the procedure is too repetitive and recommended combining the authorization and appropriations process, making the authorizing committees responsible for appropriations. However, Tower recognized, each of the twenty-nine members of the Senate Appropriations Committee has "a plum assignment, and unlike the seventy-one other Senators has an opportunity to be on four or five subcommittees, and to deal with every spending measure as it goes to the full Appropriations Committee." Tower said he realized that his proposal was not feasible, "but I am not here to advise on feasibility, but rather on what is needed." Tower also suggested that the Budget Committee be disbanded and its functions given to a smaller Appropriations Committee which would also have responsibility for appropriations matters not coverd by any authorizing committee.

Tower also proposed the creation of a super appropriations committee with ten subcommittees, each dealing with a specific area. All Senators would serve on this committee, each Senator assigned to one or two subcommittees. With this plan, most current committees would be abolished, but Foreign Relations, Finance, Rules, and Ethics would be retained. This plan would require creating three new committees on Management of Government, General Laws, and Regulated Industries.

Republican Senator Mack Mattingly of Georgia blamed the problems of the Senate on the number of committees (25), subcommittees (101), and committee staff (1,250). "Senators are spread too thinly among committee and subcommittee assignments," Mattingly testified. He pointed out that he serves on two committees, one select committee, and eleven subcommittees. "The result is that the subcommittees have become fiefdoms and private status symbols, as if the office of the United States Senator was not enough status," he said.

On September 9, 1984, a month after the committee hearings ended, Quayle discussed his findings with the *New York Times*.[7] "What I hope to do," he told the *Times*, "is put this question to the Senate: 'Do you want to change or do you really want to keep on going this way?' And if you want to go on this way, the respect for the institution is going to dwindle. We're going to have to show more self-restraint. . . . I would like to see the enforcement of a current rule that no Senator can serve on more than two major committees, such as Foreign Relations and Appropriations, and one other committee, such as Veterans. Presently fifty percent of us violate that rule."

Quayle said the number of committees and subcommittees for each Senator should be no more than eleven (some currently have as many as seventeen assignments), and the number of subcommittees for each committee, except Appropriations, should be limited to five. This would eliminate thirty-one subcommittees. He also recommended a two-year budget cycle, computerizing committee schedules, and changing rules for post-cloture procedure. The Temporary Committee issued its report to the Senate at the end of the session, and it was referred to the Senate Rules Committee—known as the graveyard of reform—for action in the new Congress.

"There's always hope for the Senate," Quayle said in the closing days of the 98th Congress. "There's a lot of frustration out there, a lot of concern about the Senate institution. We've all campaigned very hard to get to the Senate and you don't want to see the institution suffer. However, there's a great deal of dissatisfaction in the Senate with its operation. Whether that translates into votes next year is hard to say. I want to see the Senate face up to the issue, to see a vote, to have the Senate say whether it prefers all the proliferation, the mess, the duplication, or not. . . . A lot of Senators are going to have to give up something and giving up something for a politician is not an easy thing to do. It is not going to be easy to change things."

On the first day of the 99th Congress, the Temporary Committee's chairman and cochairman, Senators Quayle and Ford, introduced resolutions to amend the Senate rules in accordance with the Select Committee's report. The resolutions were referred to the Senate Rules Committee, where they remain.

However, the Temporary Committee did effect one change. Its recommendation to reverse the growth of committee and subcommittee assignments and the number of subcommittees resulted in the number of "A" committee assignments being reduced from 231 in the 98th Congress to 214 in the 99th (See Table 2). Also the total number of subcommittees of standing committees was decreased from 102 in the previous Congress to 88, the lowest number of such subcommittees since the early 1960s (See Table 3).

Senators now serve on an average of 10.75 committees, down from
11.95 in the last Congress (See Table 4).

In addition the Committee on Rules reported a resolution to
establish a committee to study a report on a two-year budget, another recommendation of the Temporary Select Committee.

"Despite these positive results," Senator Quayle told the Senate
on June 6, 1985, one year to the day that the Senate passed a
resolution to establish the Temporary Select Committee to Study
the Senate Committee System, "I must admit that the pace of pro-

**Table 2**
**Senate Committee Membership Levels\***

|  | 98th | 99th | Recommended |
|---|---|---|---|
| **"A" committees:** | | | |
| Agriculture | 18 | 17 | 15 |
| Appropriations | 29 | 29 | 27 |
| Armed Services | 18 | 19 | 15 |
| Banking | 18 | 15 | 15 |
| Commerce | 17 | 17 | 17 |
| Energy | 21 | 18 | 17 |
| Environment | 18 | 15 | 15 |
| Finance | 20 | 20 | 19 |
| Foreign Relations | 18 | 17 | 15 |
| Governmental Affairs | 18 | 13 | 13 |
| Judiciary | 18 | 18 | 17 |
| Labor | 18 | 16 | 15 |
| Totals | 231 | 214 | 200 |
| **"B" committees:** | | | |
| Budget | 22 | 22 | 21 |
| Rules | 12 | 15 | 11 |
| Small Business | 19 | 19 | 13 |
| Veterans' Affairs | 12 | 12 | 11 |
| Intelligence | 15 | 15 | 11 |
| Aging | 19 | 19 | 13 |
| Joint Economic | 10 | 10 | 10 |
| Totals | 109 | 112 | 97 |

Note.—Indian Affairs is not considered among the committees. This
committee had 7 members in the 98th Congress, and has 9 members in the
99th Congress. The recommended level was 7.

\*From the *Congressional Record*, June 6, 1985 (prepared by the Congressional
Research Service)

Table 3

## U.S. Senate, Number of Committees and their Subcommittees: 1945–1986*

| Congress | Standing committees No.[1] | Standing committees No. of subcommittees[1] | Select and special committees No.[2] | Select and special committees No. of subcommittees[2] | Joint committees No.[2] | Joint committees No. of subcommittees[2] | Total panels |
|---|---|---|---|---|---|---|---|
| 79 (1945–46) | [a]33 | [a]57 | 7 | [3]10 | 6 | [4]NA | NA |
| 80 (1947–48) | 15 | 61 | 3 | NA | 6 | NA | NA |
| 81 (1949–50) | 15 | 63 | 2 | NA | 10 | NA | NA |
| 82 (1951–52) | 15 | 65 | 3 | NA | 9 | NA | NA |
| 83 (1953–54) | 15 | 66 | 1 | NA | 10 | NA | NA |
| 84 (1955–56) | 15 | 87 | 5 | NA | 11 | 11 | NA |
| 85 (1957–58) | 16 | 85 | 4 | 4 | 9 | 12 | 130 |
| 86 (1959–60) | 16 | 87 | 5 | 0 | 12 | 8 | 128 |
| 87 (1961–62) | 16 | 88 | 2 | 0 | 11 | 6 | 129 |
| 88 (1963–64) | 16 | 85 | 3 | 6 | 11 | 13 | 134 |
| 89 (1965–66) | 16 | 92 | 3 | 6 | 11 | 14 | 142 |
| 90 (1967–68) | 16 | 98 | 5 | 6 | 11 | 15 | 157 |
| 91 (1969–70) | 16 | 101 | 5 | 12 | 10 | 15 | 159 |
| 92 (1971–72) | 17 | 115 | 5 | 12 | 8 | 15 | 173 |
| 93 (1973–74) | 18 | 127 | 7 | 13 | 9 | 16 | 190 |
| 94 (1975–76) | 18 | 122 | 6 | 13 | 7 | 14 | 180 |
| 95 (1977–78) | 15 | 96 | 6 | [5]12 | 4 | 5 | 138 |
| 96 (1979–80) | 15 | 90 | 5 | 10 | 4 | 5 | 129 |
| 97 (1981–82) | 16 | 101 | 5 | 4 | 4 | 6 | 136 |
| 98 (1983–84) | 16 | 102 | 5 | 4 | 4 | 6 | 137 |
| 99 (1985–86) | 16 | 88 | 5 | 4 | 4 | 6 | 123 |

[1] Source: Unless otherwise noted, data are compiled from U.S. Library of Congress. Congressional Research Service. Standing Committee Structure and Assignments: House and Senate. Report No. 82-42 GOV, by Sula P. Richardson and Susan Scheldrup. Washington, 1982. p. 17.

[2] Sources: Unless otherwise noted, data are compiled from Brownson, Congressional Staff Directory; Congressional Quarterly, Congressional Quarterly Almanac and CQ Weekly Report; and West Publishing Co., U.S. Code Congressional and Administrative News.

[3] U.S. Congress. Joint Committee on the Organization of Congress. Hearings, 79th Cong. 1st sess., March 13–June 29, 1945. Washington, U.S. Government Printing Office, 1945. p. 1041.

[4] This information is not readily available.

[5] Includes one three-member Ad Hoc Working Group of the Select Committee on Intelligence.

*From the *Congressional Record*, June 6, 1985 (prepared by the Congressional Research Service)

Table 4
U.S. Senate, Committee Assignments: 1945–1986*

TABLE 2.—U.S. SENATE, COMMITTEE ASSIGNMENTS: 1945–1986

| Congress | Total number of assignments | | | | | Mean number of committee assignments | | | | |
|---|---|---|---|---|---|---|---|---|---|---|
| | Standing committees[1] | Subcommittees of standing committees[1] | Select, special and joint committees[2] | Subcommittees of select, special and joint committees[2] | Total | Standing committees | Subcommittees of standing committees | Select, special and joint committees | Subcommittees of select, special and joint committees | Total panels |
| 79 (1945–46) | 489[2] | 437[3] | 98 | NA[4] | NA | 5.09 | 4.55 | 1.02 | NA | NA |
| 80 (1947–48) | 201 | 326 | 62 | NA | NA | 2.09 | 3.40 | .65 | NA | NA |
| 81 (1949–50) | 203 | 313 | 62 | NA | NA | 2.12 | 3.26 | .62 | NA | NA |
| 82 (1951–52) | 203 | 332 | 67 | NA | NA | 2.12 | 3.46 | .70 | NA | NA |
| 83 (1953–54) | 211 | 373 | 63 | NA | NA | 2.20 | 3.89 | .66 | NA | NA |
| 84 (1955–56) | 212 | 514 | 100 | 48 | 874 | 2.21 | 5.35 | 1.04 | 0.50 | 9.10 |
| 85 (1957–58) | 228 | 530 | 98 | 36 | 892 | 2.38 | 5.52 | 1.02 | .38 | 9.29 |
| 86 (1959–60) | 250 | 631 | 116 | 66 | 1,063 | 2.50 | 6.31 | 1.16 | .66 | 10.63 |
| 87 (1961–62) | 240 | 636 | 95 | 59 | 1,030 | 2.40 | 6.36 | .95 | .59 | 10.30 |
| 88 (1963–64) | 256 | 660 | 101 | 86 | 1,103 | 2.56 | 6.60 | 1.01 | .86 | 11.03 |
| 89 (1965–66) | 250 | 727 | 101 | 154 | 1,232 | 2.50 | 7.27 | 1.01 | 1.54 | 12.32 |
| 90 (1967–68) | 252 | 752 | 120 | 165 | 1,289 | 2.52 | 7.52 | 1.20 | 1.65 | 12.89 |
| 91 (1969–70) | 245 | 797 | 110 | 184 | 1,336 | 2.45 | 7.97 | 1.10 | 1.84 | 13.36 |
| 92 (1971–72) | 247 | 895 | 124 | 197 | 1,463 | 2.47 | 8.95 | 1.24 | 1.97 | 14.63 |
| 93 (1973–74) | 258 | 946 | 148 | 217 | 1,569 | 2.58 | 9.46 | 1.48 | 2.17 | 15.69 |
| 94 (1975–76) | 240 | 969 | 120 | 228 | 1,557 | 2.40 | 9.69 | 1.20 | 2.28 | 15.57 |
| 95 (1977–78) | 243 | 658 | 84 | 69 | 1,054 | 2.43 | 6.58 | .84 | .69 | 10.54 |
| 96 (1979–80) | 252 | 668 | 78 | 76 | 1,074 | 2.52 | 6.68 | .78 | .76 | 10.74 |
| 97 (1981–82) | 282 | 693 | 76 | 68 | 1,119 | 2.82 | 6.93 | .76 | .68 | 11.19 |
| 98 (1983–84) | 295[5] | 771 | 80 | 49 | 1,195 | 2.95 | 7.71 | .80 | .49 | 11.95 |
| 99 (1985–86) | 282 | 672 | 74 | 47 | 1,075 | 2.82 | 6.72 | .74 | .47 | 10.75 |

[1] Source: Unless otherwise noted, data is compiled from U.S. Library of Congress. Congressional Research Service. Standing Committee Structure and Assignments: House and Senate. Report No. 82-42 GOV, by Sula P. Richardson and Susan Schjelderup. Washington, 1982. p. 77.
[2] Sources: Unless otherwise noted, data is compiled from Brownson, Congressional Staff Director; Congressional Quarterly, Congressional Quarterly Almanac and CQ Weekly Report; and West Publishing Co., U.S. Code Congressional and Administrative News.
[3] U.S. Congress, Joint Committee on the Organization of Congress. Hearings, 79th Cong., 1st sess., March 13–June 29, 1945. Washington, U.S. Government Printing Office, 1945. pp. 1040–1041.
[4] This information is not readily available.
[5] U.S. Congress. Senate. United States Senate Telephone Directory, May, 1984. Senate Publication 98-21, 98th Cong. 2nd Sess. Washington, U.S. Government Printing Office, 1984. pp. 77–120.

*From the *Congressional Record*, June 6, 1985 (prepared by the Congressional Research Service) gress has been glacial and that the prospects for meaningful action in the Congress becomes ever more remote. . . . The time for reform is before we tie ourselves in procedural knots—and that time is disappearing.[8]

> Reform is easy to talk about, but hard to achieve. So is change.
> —Senator Howard Baker

## Notes

1. Established in June 1984.
2. *Congressional Record*, 98th Cong., 2d sess., 1984, 130, No. 75.
3. See Allen Schick, "The Three-Ring Circus," in Mann and Ornstein, *The New Congress*, p. 311–28.
4. *Congressional Record*, 98th Cong., 2d sess., 1984, 130, No. 75.
5. U.S. Senate, transcript of proceedings, Hearings of the Temporary Select Committee to Study the Senate Committee System, 98th Cong., 2d sess., 31 July 1984, p. 7.
6. See Chapter 2.
7. *New York Times*, September 9, 1984, p. 45.
8. *Congressional Record*, 99th Cong., 1st sess., 1985, 131, No. 74. S 7681-82.

# Bibliography

## Books

Bailey, Stephen K. *Congress in the Seventies.* New York: St. Martin's Press, 1970.

Bibby, John, and Davidson, Roger. *On Capitol Hill.* New York: Holt, Rinehart and Winston, 1967.

Bolling, Richard. *House Out of Order.* New York: E. P. Dutton and Co., 1985.

———. *Power in the House.* New York: E. P. Dutton and Co., 1974.

Cater, Douglass. *Power in Washington.* New York: Random House, 1964.

Committee for Economic Development. *Making Congress More Effective.* New York: Committee for Economic Development, 1970.

*Congressional Quarterly, Congress Reconsidered,* 3d ed. Washington, D.C.: Congressional Quarterly, Inc., 1985.

———. *Guide to Congress,* 3d ed. Washington, D.C.: Congressional Quarterly, Inc., 1982.

———. *How Congress Works,* Washington, D.C.: Congressional Quarterly, Inc., 1983.

Evins, Joe. L. *Understanding Congress.* New York: Clarkson, N. Potter, Inc., 1963.

Fenno, Richard F., Jr. *Congressmen in Committees.* Boston: Little, Brown and Co., 1973.

———. *The Power of the Purse.* Boston: Little, Brown and Co., 1973.

Fishel, Jeff. *Party and Opposition.* New York: David McKay, 1973.

Foley, Michael. *The New Senate.* New Haven: Yale University Press, 1980.

Fox, Harrison, W., Jr., and Susan Webb Hammond. *Congressional Staffs.* New York: The Free Press, 1977.

Goodwin, George. *The Little Legislatures: Committees of Congress*. Amherst: University of Massachusetts Press, 1970.

Green, Mark J., Fallows, James, and Swick, David. *Who Runs Congress*. New York: Bantam, 1972.

Hinckley, Barbara. *The Seniority System in Congress*. Bloomington: University of Indiana Press, 1971.

Jewell, Malcom, and Patterson, Samuel C. *The Legislative Process in the United States*. New York: Random House, 1966.

Jones, Charles O. *The Minority Party in Congress*. Boston: Little, Brown and Co., 1970.

Keefe, William J., and Ogul, Morris S. *The American Legislative Process: Congress and the States*, 3d ed. Englewood Cliffs, N.J.: Prentice-Hall, 1972.

Kingdon, John R. *Congressmen's Voting Decisions*. New York: Harper and Row, 1973.

Lees, John D. *The Committee System of the United States Congress*. London: Routledge and Kegan Paul, 1967.

McNeil, Neil. *Forge of Democracy: the House of Representatives*. New York: David McKay, 1969.

Mann, Thomas E., and Ornstein, Norman J., eds. *The New Congress*. Washington, D.C.: American Enterprise Institute for Public Policy Research, 1981.

Morrow, William L. *Congressional Committees*. New York: Charles Scribner's Sons, 1969.

Peabody, Robert. *Leadership in Congress*. Boston: Little, Brown, and Company, 1976.

Polsby, Nelson, ed. *Congressional Behavior*. New York: Random House, 1970.

Reed, T. R. *Congressional Odyssey*. San Francisco: W. H. Freeman & Co., 1980.

Riddick, Floyd M. *The United States Congress: Organization and Procedure*. Manassas, Va.: National Capitol Publishers, Inc., 1949.

Ripley, Randall. *Majority Party Leadership in Congress*. Boston: Little, Brown and Co., 1969

———. *Party Leaders in the House of Representatives*. Washington, D.C.: The Brookings Institute, 1967.

———. *Power in the Senate*. New York: St. Martin's Press, 1969.

Tacheron, Donald G., and Udall, Morris K. *The Job of the Congressman*. Indianapolis: Bobbs-Merrill Co., Inc. 1966.

Vogler, David. *The Politics of Congress*. Boston: Allyn and Bacon, 1974.

Weaver, Warren, Jr. *Both Your Houses*. New York: Praeger, 1972.

## Articles

Abram, Michael, and Cooper, Joseph. "The Rise of Seniority in the House of Representatives." *Polity* 1 (Fall 1968).

Balch, Stephen H. "Getting That Extra Edge: Seniority and Early Appointments to the U.S. Senate." *Polity* 11 (Fall 1978).

Berg, John C. "The Effects of Seniority Reform on Three House Committees in the 94th Congress." In Leroy N. Rieselback, ed. *Legislative Reform: The Policy Impact* (Lexington, Mass.: Heath, 1978).

———. "Reforming Seniority in the House of Representatives: Did It Make Any Difference?" *Policy Studies Journal* 5 (Summer 1977).

Cavanagh, Thomas E. "The Dispersion of Authority in the House of Representatives." *Political Science Quarterly* 97 (Winter 1982–1983).

Cohen, David. "The Continuing Challenge of Congressional Reform." *Democratic Review* 1 (1975).

Cohen, Richard E. "The 96th Congress: Who'll Be Calling The Shots?" *National Journal* 10 (November 1978).

*Congressional Quarterly*. "Bolling Committee: Members Reforming House System." *Congressional Quarterly Weekly Report*, 24 November 1973.

———. "Challenges of Seniority System by Both Parties." *Congressional Quarterly Weekly Report*. 15 January 1971.

———. "Congressional Seniority: A Crusty Tradition." *Congressional Quarterly Weekly Report*, 6 January 1973.

———. "Democrats to Increase Hold on House Committees." *Congressional Quarterly Weekly Report*, 6 November 1982.

———. "New Setbacks for House Seniority System." *Congressional Quarterly Weekly Report*, 3 February 1979.

———. "Seniority Rule: Change in Procedure, Not in Practice." *Congressional Quarterly Weekly Report*, 27 January 1973.

———. "Standing in Line: Behind Scenes Jockeying for Committees Posts. . . . " *Congressional Quarterly Weekly Report*, 18 November 1978.

Democratic Study Group. "The Seniority System in the U.S. House of Representatives." Washington, D.C.: Democratic Study Group, 1970.

Evans, Medford. "Chairman: Our Powerful Feudal Chieftains." *American Opinion* 17 (July–August 1974).

Farnsworth, David N., and Stanga, John E. "Seniority, Reform and Democratic Committee Assignments in the House of Representatives." *Policy Studies Journal* 5 (Summer 1977).

Fowler, Linda L. "The Electoral Effects of House Committee Assignments." *Journal of Politics* 42 (February 1980).

Goldstein, Dan, and Scamell, Richard. "Congressional Seniority and Unequal Representation: A Proposal for Reform." *Texas Law Review* 51 (April 1973).

Hinckley, Barbara. "Seniority 1975: Old Theories Confront New Facts." *British Journal of Political Science* 6 (October 1976).

Hopkins, Bruce R. "Congressional Reform Advances in the 93rd Congress." *American Bar Association Journal*, January 1974.

House Select Committee on Committees, U.S. Congress. *Committee Reorganization in the House*. 93rd Cong., 2d sess. Washington, D.C.: Government Printing Office, 1974.

Kostroski, Warren. "The Effects of Number of Terms on the Re-election of Senators, 1920–1970." *Journal of Politics* 40 (May 1978).

Lambro, Donald. "The Great Seniority Struggle—Can Congress Survive?" *Rally*, July–August 1967. Reprinted in the *Congressional Record*, 29 September 1967.

Malbin, Michael J. "Congress Report 'House Democrats Oust Senior Members from Power' " *National Journal* 25 January 1975.

Mansfield, Harvey C., Sr. "The Dispersion of Authority in Congress." New York: Proceedings of the Academy of Political Science, 32, no. 1, 1975.

Nathanson, Eric. "The Caucus vs. the Barons" *The Nation*, 11 January 1975.

Polsby, Nelson W., and Miriam Gallagher. "Growth of the Seniority System in the U.S. House of Representatives." *American Political Science Review* 63 (September 1969).

Ray, Bruce. "Committee Attractiveness in the U.S. House, 1963–1981." *American Journal of Political Science* 26 (August 1982).

Walsh, John. "Reform in the House: Amending the Seniority Rule." *Science* 179 (March 1973).

## Interviews

Former Senator James O. Abourezk (D., South Dakota), September 28, 1983.

Morris Amitay, former head of AIPAC (American Israel Public Affairs Committee), and former House and Senate professional staff, September 19, 1983.

Former Congressman Richard Bolling (D., Missouri), January 9, 1981.

Alan Boyd, former Department of Transportation Secretary (administration of President Lyndon B. Johnson), October 17, 1983.

Mace Broide, staff director, House Budget Committee, and former administrative assistant to Senator Vance Hartke. (D., Indiana), June 3, 1980.

Senator Dale Bumpers (D., Arkansas), December 7, 1983.

Senator Quentin Burdick (N., Dakota), January 6, 1981.

Senator Robert Byrd (D., West Virginia), February 27, 1984.

Senator Lawton Chiles (D., Florida), February 9, 1984.

Former Senator Frank Church (D., Idaho), September 29, 1983.

Robert Clark, congressional correspondent, ABC News, October 5, 1983.

Former Congressman Barber Conable (R., New York), March 1, 1984.

Former Senator Marlow Cook (R., Kentucky), September 20, 1983.

Harley Dirks, former aide to Senator Warren Magnuson (D., Washington), April 26, 1980.

Paul Duke, WETA Washington correspondent, and former NBC News and *Wall Street Journal* congressional reporter, March 1, 1984.

Former Congresswoman Millicent Fenwick (R., New Jersey), January 7, 1981.

Charles Ferris, former chief counsel to the Senate Democratic Policy Committee and former chairman of the Federal Communications Commission, October 6, 1983.

James E. Guirard, former administrative assistant to Senator Allen J. Ellender (D., Louisiana) and Russell B. Long (D., Louisiana), Mary 20, 1980.

Former Senator William Hathaway (D., Maine), November 9, 1983.

George Herman, CBS TV Washington correspondent, October 11, 1983.

William Hildenbrand, former Secretary of the Senate, May 14, 1980.

F. Nordy Hoffman, former Senate Sergeant at Arms, June 19, 1980.

John Horne, former aide to Senator John Sparkman (D., Alabama), and former head of the Small Business Administration, January 6, 1981.

Former Congressman Frank Ikard (D., Texas), January 31, 1984.

Mary Irwin, formerly professional staff, Senate Judiciary Committee, January 8, 1981.

Herb Jasper, telecommunications industry lobbyist and former Senate Budget Committee aide, October 21, 1983.

Haynes Johnson, Pulitzer Price winning reporter, the *Washington Post*, November 11, 1983.

Former Congressman Joe Karth (D., Minnesota), January 8, 1981.

Tom Kerester, former counsel to the House Ways and Means Committee, January 9, 1981.

J. Stanley Kimmitt, former Secretary of the Senate, June 4, 1980.

Tom C. Korologos, former White House Congressional Liaison for President Richard Nixon, and former press secretary to Senator Wallace Bennett (R., Utah), September 16, 1983.

Former Congressman and Defense Secretary Melvin R. Laird (R., Wisconsin), October 19, 1983.

Former Senator Eugene McCarthy (D., Minnesota), October 14, 1983.

Senator James McClure (R., Idaho), December 2, 1983.

John McConnell, former aide to (then Senate Majority Whip) Russell B. Long (D., Louisiana), June 18, 1980.

Former Senator Gale McGee (D., Wyoming), December 22, 1983.

Former Congressman George Mahon (D., Texas), Chairman, House Appropriations Committee, July 31, 1979.

Mike Michaelson, vice-president of C-Span Cable Broadcasting, and former Superintendent of the House Radio-Television Gallery, September 9, 1983.

Nicholas Miller, formerly on staff of Senator Magnuson (D., Washington), former counsel to Senate Commerce Committee, and formerly on President Carter's White House staff, October 12, 1983.

Wilbur Mills (D., Arkansas), former Chairman of the House Ways and Means Committee, September 27, 1983.

Tracy Mullin, former aide to Senate Minority Leader Hugh Scott (R., Pennsylvania), October 10, 1983.

Richard Murphy, former aide to Senate Minority Leader Hugh Scott, June 18, 1980.

Former Senator Gaylord Nelson (D., Wisconsin), October 3, 1983.

Patrick O'Donnell, former White House Congressional Liaison (Presidents Richard Nixon and Gerald Ford), September 28, 1983.

Steve Paradise, former staff director, chief counsel, Senate Labor Committee, May 14, 1980.

Michael Pertschuk, former chief counsel, Senate Commerce Committee, and former Federal Trade Commission Chairman (administration of President Jimmy Carter), October 21, 1983.

Don Phillips, House Bureau Chief, United Press International, September 22, 1983.

Former Congressman W. R. Poage (D., Texas), August 1, 1979.

Senator William Proxmire (D., Wisconsin), October 9, 1983.

Senator Dan Quayle (R., Indiana), September 20, 1984.

Dr. Floyd Riddick, Senate Parliamentarian Emeritus, April 15, 1980.

Former Congressman Paul Rogers (D., Florida), Chairman of the House Health Subcommittee, October 17, 1983.

Maurice Rosenblatt, Washington lobbyist, October 4, 1983.

Former Senate Minority Leader Hugh Scott (R., Pennsylvania), October 13, 1983.

Samuel Shaffer, retired chief congressional correspondent for *Newsweek* magazine, October 13, 1983.

Frank Silbey, former investigator for House and Senate oversight committees, September.

Grover Smith, former press secretary to Senator John Sparkman (D., Alabama), June 9, 1980.

Jack Sullivan, former administrative assistant to Congressman Clement Zablocki (D., Wisconsin), January 8, 1981.

Former Senator Robert Taft (R., Ohio), November 15, 1983.

Wayne Thevenot, former legislative assistant to Senator Russell B. Long (D., Louisiana), April 15, 1980.

Dan Thomasson, Washington Bureau Chief, Scripps-Howard Newspapers, September 14, 1983.

Congressman Morris Udall (D., Arizona), March 22, 1984.

Fred Wertheimer, President, Common Cause, January 29, 1980.

Anthony Zagami, counsel to the Joint Committee on Printing, and former counsel to the Secretary of the Senate, September 23, 1983.

# Index

Bumpers, Dale: on aging committee chairmen, 37; on becoming a
committee chairman, 59–60; on
change in Congress, 52; on limiting debate time and time Senators spend on the floor, 25–26;
on limiting the number of terms
of members of Congress, 99; on
party discipline and leadership,
61–62; on periodic elections of
chairmen of committees, 95; on
scheduling congressional sessions, 24, 25; on seniority system, 37, 40; on upper age limits, 98
Burdick, Quentin, on the seniority
system, 29
Bureaucracy, congressional staff as,
88–89
Byrd, Robert C.: on campaigning
costs, 22–23; on changes in Senate, 46–47; on Congress and the
Republic, 14; on importance of
committee assignments to members of Congress, 59; on new independence in senators, 48; on
the seniority system, 29–30

Campaign committees, 61
Campaign contributions, 86
Campaigning costs, 21–23
Cannon, Joseph G., 4–5
Caucuses, 8, 9, 56, 100; approval
of committee chairmen by, 45;
before open committee sessions,
50
Cellers, Emanuel, 47
Chairmanships, limit to number of
a Senator's, 87 n.5
Chiles, Lawton: on Congress and
representative government, 14–
15; on leadership by Congress,
16; on national vs. state issues,

58; on PACs, 51; on power of
committee chairmen, 46; on the
seniority system, 30, 43–44
Church, Frank: on campaign financing, 22; on emasculation of
congressional leadership, 63–64;
on increased activity of freshmen
Senators, 63; on members of
Congress being overwhelmed by
their staffs, 91; on seniority system, 28; on subcommittees, 78–
79, 81
Civil rights bills killed by Senator
Eastland, 37
Clark, Robert: on costs of increasing congressional staffs, 91; on
improvement in competence of
members of Congress, 47; on
new members of Congress as
subcommittee chairmen, 77; on
subcommittees, 80
Clay, Henry, as Speaker of the
House, 4
Committee assignment in the
House, 4–5, 55, 56, 73–74
Committee assignment in the Senate, 5–6, 55–58; limits on, 87
n.5, 106, 109–10
Committee assignment procedures, 55–56
Committee assignments: Democratic, in the House, 60 n.3, 71,
73; factors considered in, 56; importance of, to members of Congress, 59–60; the Johnson Rule
and, 68; obtaining, 56–58
Committee chairmen: accountability and selection of, 9; ages of,
7; aging of, 37–39; autocratic,
34–37, 94; caucus approval of,
45; Democratic caucus rule on
secret ballot on, 9; effect of subcommittees on, 82–84; as *ex of-*

of Congress and Senator Baker's
idea of a citizen legislature, 25;
on the seniority system, 31–32;
on staff members doing work of
members of Congress, 91; on
sunshine laws, 49–50
Public opinion, lawmakers and, 16

Quayle, Dan, 104–7
Quayle Committee on Senate committee system, 104–7

Rayburn, Sam, 64–66
Reelection: seniority and, 32; as
true test of a politician, 34
Reform(s): aims of the most serious, 94; attacking Ways and
Means Committee, 73–74;
"Hansen II," 9, 10; "Hansen III,"
10–11; movement for, 104; party
discipline weakened by, 100;
pressure for, from outside Congress, 8; reforming the, 102
Representatives: lengthening terms
of, 17; minimum age for, 97
Republican Caucus, 56
Republican Committee on Committees, 56
Republican Conference, secret ballot election of each ranking minority member of committees
and, 8
Revenues, control over, by House
Appropriations Committee, 70
Riddick, Floyd: on Senate Judiciary Committee Chairman James
O. Eastland, 37; on Senator
Richard Russell, 39; on special
interest groups, 51
Rogers, Paul: on financing of elec-
tions, 21; on overthrow of three
House committee chairmen, 11–
12; on political independence of

politicians, 63; on seniority system, 40; on subcommittees, 78
Roll call votes: limiting, 23; party
discipline and, 63–64
Rosenblatt, Maurice: on F. Edward Herbert, 36; on House
Armed Services Committee
chairman Carl Vinson, 35–36; on
House Rules Committee Chairman Judge Smith, 35; on sur-
vival under the seniority system,
32; on Wilbur Mills, 71
Rostenkowski, Dan, 75
Rules Committee of the House:
clearing of legislation by, 42 n.2;
nomination and appointment to,
56; power of, 35; Ways and
Means Committee and, 73
Russell, Richard, 39

Safe districts, seniority and, 32–34
Satterfield, David E., III, 85
Scott, Hugh: on aging committee
chairmen, 38; on cross-jurisdictional claims of subcommittees,
81; on House Armed Services
Committee Chairman Carl Vinson, 36; on increasing the number of subcommittees, 80; on
Sam Rayburn, 65; on scheduling
sessions of Congress, 24; on
Senator Richard Russell, 39; on
the seniority system, 31
Senate: bills rewritten on floor of,
43; budget–authorizations–appropriations cycle and, 106; circumventing the committee system in, 43; committee
assignments in, 113; as deliberative body of Congress, 108; di-
luting power of senior members
of, 67; floor procedure changes
proposed, 106–7; Johnson's

## About the Author and Editor

MAURICE B. TOBIN had served for five years as counsel and legislative assistant to the chairman of the Public Works and Transportation Committee of Congress when he left to establish the Washington law firm of Tobin and French and to broaden his civic and public service. He was a U.S. delegate to the United Nations Plenipotentiary Telecommunications Conference in Nairobi in 1982, and has been a presidential appointee to the Executive Exchange Commission. As a civic leader and volunteer, he chaired the successful seven-year effort to save and restore Washington's historic National Theater. His government experience, special legal studies, technological interests, frequent lectures on public affairs, and numerous civic contributions have given him an unusual perspective on Washington and enable him to maintain an active academic, international, and entrepreneurial career.

JOAN SHAFFER is a writer, editor, photographer, and media relations specialist who has worked in the non-profit sector, private industry, and government. Her congressional and political experience includes seven years as deputy press secretary to Senator Russell B. Long, three years as assistant press secretary to Senator Fred R. Harris, and one year as a media assistant in the national headquarters of Senator Barry Goldwater's presidential campaign. Currently she directs communications for Democrats for the 80's, an independent political committee.